Contents

The Open University

U116

Environment: journeys through a changing world

Block 6
Cities and sustainability

Parts 1–3

Bob Everett, Godfrey Boyle and Roger Blackmore

This publication forms part of the Open University course U116 *Environment: journeys through a changing world*. Details of this and other Open University courses can be obtained from the Student Registration and Enquiry Service, The Open University, PO Box 197, Milton Keynes MK7 6BJ, United Kingdom (tel. +44 (0)845 300 60 90; email general-enquiries@open.ac.uk).

Alternatively, you may visit the Open University website at www.open.ac.uk where you can learn more about the wide range of courses and packs offered at all levels by The Open University.

To purchase a selection of Open University course materials visit www.ouw.co.uk, or contact Open University Worldwide, Walton Hall, Milton Keynes MK7 6AA, United Kingdom for a brochure (tel. +44 (0)1908 858793; fax +44 (0)1908 858787; email ouw-customer-services@open.ac.uk).

The Open University
Walton Hall, Milton Keynes
MK7 6AA

First published 2010.

Copyright © 2010 The Open University

Edited and designed by The Open University.

Typeset by SR Nova Pvt. Ltd, Bangalore, India.

Printed and bound in the United Kingdom by Halstan Printing Group, Amersham.

ISBN 978 0 7492 2565 0

1.1

Introduction to Block 6

Block 6 is called 'Cities and sustainability'. It represents the final stage of your exploration of our changing world, a homecoming so to speak, and is an appropriate place to review the journey so far.

U116 is about our environment, our planet: the physical world, the land, oceans and atmosphere, and the web of life that inhabits it and interacts with it. It is about the connections and flows that occur between and within these two components of our environment. These interconnections create a changing world. Change is natural. But one species – humans – through its social organisations and its use of technologies is affecting the world dramatically and thereby changing these physical flows and ecological networks. In particular, the world is now warming rapidly and biodiversity is heading for another mass extinction.

U116 is also about our story: how people and societies are living with, responding to, trying to understand and cope with the changing world arising from our many impacts on the planet. This raises many questions: what kinds of economic activity and social organisation, lifestyles and growth, ways of managing ourselves and our environment should we follow to allow our children the same or better opportunities than we have had? In other words, how can we live more sustainably?

These two threads, *connections* and *change*, run through the course, together with the question 'how can we live more sustainably?', to which there is not one answer but many.

A major purpose of Block 6 *Cities and sustainability* is to explore how we can live more sustainably, both individually and as societies; but why the focus on cities? One compelling reason is that most of the world now lives and/ or works in towns or cities. In 2008 humanity passed a significant milestone: over half of the global population of 6.6 billion now live in cities. In the continents of Europe, North and South America and Australia, three-quarters of the populations are already urban. Over the next 50 years the populations of Asia and Africa are likely to complete a similar transition to city life. During this time the world population is projected to increase to 9 billion, but much of the increase will be concentrated in cities because migration from the country to the city is expected to continue.

Although cities and towns and the people who live in them occupy only 3% of the world's land area their global impact is immense. They already account for much of the world's production, consumption and waste generation. For example, according to the United Nations (quoted in Ash et al., 2008) they are responsible for 75% of global energy consumption and 80% of greenhouse gas emissions (and take most of the goods made in China). The way cities manage their affairs, and the way their citizens behave, has a global impact not only on ecosystems and biodiversity but also on how societies organise themselves. Cities are the seats of power and influence and often contain within their growing spheres of influence extremes of both affluence and poverty. They are the 'cauldrons of change' and the entry point for the flows of migrating humanity and ideas. Individuals, regions and nations often define themselves by the state and status of their cities. If we are to take responsibility for our impact on the planet we should begin by looking at what is happening in our own 'backyard'; we have to look at urban living.

> Preserving the rights of our children and grandchildren to health and happiness depends on what we do today about global environmental change. The battle for a sustainable environmental future is being waged primarily in the world's cities. Right now, cities draw together many of Earth's major environmental problems: population growth, pollution, resource degradation and waste generation.

> *(United Nations Populations Fund, 2007)*

While the topic of this block is cities, the course journey focuses on a single city, London, for many of its examples and detailed discussions. Why the choice of London? It was the first and pre-eminent global city of the industrial age and remains today a major world city. As it grew rapidly in the nineteenth and twentieth centuries it was confronted by a range of environmental challenges and problems that many other cities and towns in North America and Europe subsequently faced. In order to continue developing it had to find solutions to several pressing environmental problems, in particular how to manage its waste and pollution. Similar challenges are today affecting many rapidly growing cities in the developing world. Solutions that were found then can still inform today's issues.

However, the world's cities now face new environmental challenges, some from global climate change and some of a more local nature. Major challenges include how to reduce the impact of cities on a rapidly warming planet while trying to reduce their vulnerability to its consequences, including heatwaves and rising sea level. Local issues include coping with new forms of pollution and caring for changing biodiversity. Many cities across the world have joined together in initiatives to learn from each other while developing their particular local solutions. As a world city whose inhabitants have deep connections to many parts of the globe, London has been in the forefront of this movement. It has also suffered its fair share of disasters from both 'old' environmental problems and new ones. It thus provides plenty of material to explore how we might all live more sustainably in the future.

Part 1 describes how authorities in London responded to two major environmental crises of water and air pollution by making major changes to the city's infrastructure. It describes the events that finally led to action and shows how this can inform some of today's challenges in cities. Part 2 concentrates on the current plans and measures that cities are taking to reduce their climate change impact by using energy more sustainably. It focuses in particular on plans to reduce London's carbon footprint. Part 3 looks to the future, comparing bold plans for eco-cities with the 'greening' of existing cities, then exploring how cities need to adapt to the environmental challenge of a warmer world by preparing for heat waves and floods, but also by promoting biodiversity. The block (and the course) ends by asking what role individuals, communities, business and government can play in a sustainable future.

In essence Block 6 tries to show that people can always find creative and positive solutions to difficult problems (and be prepared for new problems) using cities for its material. In that spirit one source of positive inspiration may come from an unlikely source: the extraordinary journey described in Block 2 *Arctic approach*. In September 1893 the Norwegian explorer Fridtjof Nansen and a crew of thirteen steered their ship *Fram* into the Arctic ice off Siberia with the intention of being held fast by it and drifting towards the North Pole. In its day this was a journey every bit as challenging and dangerous as the space missions to the moon of the 1960s and 1970s (but without the support and guidance from a mission control) and had similarly mixed motives: a combination of scientific curiosity, national pride and personal glory. Just as the Apollo missions captured our imagination and changed how we viewed the world (the views of Earth from space), Nansen's accounts did the same for the Arctic. Although the expedition did not quite run to plan, all the expedition members returned home safely after three years on the ice.

The stay on the ice was prepared for carefully. The ship carried provisions for five years on the ice, including many tonnes of petroleum and kerosene for cooking and heating in addition to coal for the ship's engines. But it also experimented with the latest technology, as these excerpts from Nansen's account of the voyage explain.

> It may be mentioned as an improvement on former expeditions that the Fram was furnished with an electric light installation. The dynamo was to be driven by the engine while we were under steam; while the intention was to drive it partly by means of the wind, partly by hand power, during our sojourn in the ice. For this purpose we took a windmill with us, and also a 'horse-mill' to be worked by ourselves. I had anticipated that this latter might have been useful in giving us exercise in the long polar night. We found, however, that there were plenty of other things to do, and we never used it; on the other hand, the windmill proved extremely serviceable.
>
> *(Nansen, 1898, p. 72)*

In October 1893 the new device was finally tested.

> It is quickly getting darker. The sun stands lower and lower every time we see it; soon it will disappear altogether, if it has not done so already. The long, dark winter is upon us, and glad shall we be to see the spring; but nothing matters much if we could only begin to move north. There is now south-westerly wind, and the windmill, which has been ready for several days, has been tried at last and works splendidly. We have beautiful electric light to-day, though the wind has not been especially strong (5–8 [metres] per second). Electric lamps are a grand institution. What a strong influence light has on one's spirits! There was a noticeable brightening-up at the dinner-table to-day; the light acted on our spirits like a draught of good wine. And how festive the saloon looks!

(Nansen, 1898, p. 269)

He later went on deck to admire by moonlight the ship held fast on the ice.

> Wonderful moonshine this evening, light as day; and along with it aurora borealis, yellow and strange in the white moonlight; a large ring round the moon – all this over the great stretch of white, shining ice, here and there in our neighbourhood piled up high by the pressure. And in the midst of this silent silvery ice-world the windmill sweeps round its dark wings against the deep-blue sky and the aurora. A strange contrast: civilisation making a sudden incursion into this frozen ghostly world.

(Nansen, 1898, p. 241)

This image can perhaps serve as inspiration, even today. If the explorers on the *Fram* were able to plan and use renewable energy in such hostile conditions, surely a hundred years later our vastly more sophisticated civilisations can make similar decisive moves?

Part 1
Cities and environmental problems past

Bob Everett and Roger Blackmore

Introduction

1

In Part 1 we look at cities, firstly reflecting on what they are and why they are so important in human society. Then we go on to look at London, and in particular London past. It was one of the first cities to enjoy the 'benefits' of the Industrial Revolution in the nineteenth century. It also had to deal with the pollution consequences: a sewage-choked River Thames culminating in the 'Great Stink' of 1858 and a longer-term problem of swirling 'pea-soup' smog. These are issues that face many cities around the world today but have been 'solved', for the moment at least, in London. We look at what lessons can be drawn in dealing with these past environmental problems that might be useful in tackling today's problem of climate change, the subject of Part 2.

1.1   What is a city?

This section explores cities from the point of view of an interested enquirer, not that of an expert. It looks briefly at several aspects of cities: their history, their connections to flows of people and materials, their resilience and vulnerability, and different models of what a city is. It then suggests that to make cities sustainable we need to think again about what cities are and the use we make of them. Although the focus of this block is cities, many of the ideas discussed here apply to the whole of modern urban society, whether people live in cities, towns or villages.

What is a city? If I was asked to describe in a sentence what a city is, what would I say? My first thought is that a city is a place where there are a large number of people living and working in close proximity, but also plenty of buildings, often large ones. Thinking about the people and buildings for a minute, I would make a distinction between two main types of building: the places where people live – housing; and places where people work, go to buy things or to relax – offices and factories, shops, cinemas and museums. In addition, there are transport links, roads and vehicles, and a host of other services that are less obvious to the eye but just as important: drinking water, sewers, power for heating and lighting, and communications. These form the basic physical and organisational support structure of a city, known as its infrastructure.

Putting this into a sentence I could say: *A city is a place with many buildings, supported by infrastructure, where large numbers of people live, work and relax.* The phrase 'a place with many buildings, supported by infrastructure' sounds awkward, but can be replaced by the term 'built environment'. My sentence now reads: *A city is a built environment where large numbers of people live, work and relax.* This description feels reasonable as a first attempt.

You might point out that this description could apply equally to towns as well as cities, or that in England the title of 'city' is only conferred by Royal Charter, while in the United States a city refers to a town with its own government and administration established by state charter (Collins, 1979). In these two countries there is a clear process for designating cities, but in others the main feature distinguishing towns from cities could be simply the population size.

Activity 1.1   Describing a city

When you think of a city, what images, what words are conjured up? Figure 1.1 shows a few examples of images, but your experience might be quite different. Make a list of the key words that come to mind if you were asked to describe a city or town that you know.

Discussion

Each city and town is unique, but they also share many common features that attract people to them but also make them wary. Typical descriptions would include words such as *modern*, *dynamic*, *affluent*, *rich*, *poor*, *uncaring*, *hard*, *anonymous*, *diverse*, *buzzing*, *busy*, *tiring*, *cool*, *exciting*, *dangerous* and *polluted*. Often cities seem to be places of rapid change; they have areas of extreme poverty and affluence living side by side, are both tiring and exciting, dynamic but dangerous. They appear to contain an intense mixture of extremes and contradictions. This might be expected when so many people from different backgrounds work and live together.

1.1.1   Cities ancient and modern

Today, as the Introduction to this block stated, the majority of the world's population is urban: it lives in towns and cities, and the trend to urban living is growing all the time. Although cities have been with us for many thousands of years, until very recently most people have lived and worked on the land, not in cities. Ancient cities such as Rome, Baghdad, Athens or Carthage have been mostly associated with successful nation states or empires and have generally flourished or fallen along with them. They have been found from Africa to Asia and Central America to Europe. They served as administrative centres for their societies and had to maintain good communication and trading links with their empires. This usually meant reliance on water transport and, for that reason, many were sited on major rivers or by a sheltered coast where ships and boats could bring and send goods and pass on news. Also, many city inhabitants relied on surplus food collected from the countryside because they no longer worked directly on the land. Cities are intimately connected with the development of agriculture and the surplus food it creates; they did not and cannot exist without it. Cities thus tended to be located close to both fertile

Figure 1.1 Images of cities: (a) commuters; (b) high-rise buildings; (c) shanty town; (d) market

lands and fresh water for food, drinking and cooking, and to have good communication links. An ideal site was near the flood plain or estuary of a river, which usually gave access to the sea.

In medieval times, improvements in agricultural productivity in parts of Europe and Asia allowed more cities to flourish. Some, such as Salisbury or Norwich in England, were based on wealth from wool, while others, such as Antwerp or Venice depended on international commerce and trade backed up by naval power. However, in Europe and North America the face of cities changed dramatically in the nineteenth century as a consequence of the Industrial Revolution. In Britain, for example, labour was needed for the new factories and mills of industrial towns and was drawn from the surrounding countryside and further afield, while ports such as Bristol, Glasgow and Liverpool grew rapidly as they traded goods and materials with countries around the world. Initially, large masses of people had to live close to their workplaces in polluted, unhealthy and crowded living conditions. In the second half of the century new transport networks, particularly the railways, allowed towns and cities to grow rapidly as new settlements including suburbs spread out from the centre alongside the railways. Spectacular growth also occurred in the capitals of the European empires, such as Paris and London.

The modern shape of cities, of central districts with skyscrapers growing ever higher, surrounded by sprawling suburbs, slums and satellite towns, developed first in the USA early in the twentieth century. Suburbia spread outwards in response to transport; first trains and trams, then buses, lorries and cars. Today, most of the growth and spread of cities is taking place in developing countries, in Asia, Africa and South America, where the speed and scale of urban transformation is remarkable. A particular feature of most modern cities, especially the more affluent ones, is how many of the materials and goods they use and consume are sourced from all over the globe, as the examples from China in Block 5 showed. Cities in the nineteenth century also imported and traded some raw materials, food and clothing globally but, with the exception of a few major centres such as London, not to the extent that occurs today.

Activity 1.2   Factors that have influenced the development of cities

This very brief (and incomplete) account of the development of cities over time has pointed to several factors that seem to be necessary for cities to develop and flourish. Outline what you think are the main factors.

Discussion
My list is:

1 Early cities needed thriving nation states or empires.

2 Their inhabitants rely on surplus food from surrounding areas and the availability of fresh water.

3 They need good communications and transport links (hence they are often found near rivers or coasts).

4 They use and trade a range of materials and goods with other parts of the world.

The first factor refers to the role of early cities as administrative centres and seats of power. In the past, when a nation or society declined or was conquered, their leading cities sometimes disappeared with them. Today, this factor mainly applies to capital cities of nations or major regions, and while states and nations still form and re-form, their cities seem to survive or rise again from the ashes of war and bombardment. In this sense, modern cities are remarkably resilient to pressure from changing economic and political circumstances, even when their populations have suffered badly.

1.1.2   A second view of the city

The other three factors relate more to geography than to history or politics. They are mainly concerned with the flow or movement of materials and people in and out of cities. To see how these factors can enrich our understanding of what a city is, return for a moment to my initial description of a city:

A city is a built environment where large numbers of people live, work and relax.

Now, instead of conjuring up an impression of the city, change your focus to what people do in a city.

Activity 1.3   Life in the city

Imagine you are meeting up for lunch in a city or town centre with a friend. You may well feel a sense of anticipation in meeting your friend and be looking forward to the buzz of the city and what it can offer. But to enjoy its attractions you rely on a number of goods and services to make your trip and have your lunch. Think of what they might be, then make a list.

Discussion
You might decide to dress up for this occasion, but even if you don't you will need to wear something! Then you have to get to the city and to the place where you will meet your friend. This could involve many possible forms of transport, from cars, buses, trains and metros to bicycles and walking. The first four need fuel to keep them going and people to run and maintain them, but even if you walk or cycle you rely on a network of roads and paths and traffic control systems, all of which require both regular maintenance by people and materials. Once you are in your cafe or restaurant, having phoned ahead to check where your friend is, you consume food and drink, which has to be brought in, prepared and then served. The restaurant itself will use lighting, heating in cold weather and equipment to cook food and, in addition, it needs to maintain its furniture and decor and provide toilets. When you have finished you pay, using cash or a card, and your table will be cleared up after you and any waste will be disposed of.

In other words, just to meet up for lunch you make use of a large array of materials, facilities and services – many of which most people take for granted but would soon notice if they were not functioning smoothly. This example of what people *do* in an urban society provides a clearer picture of a city as a place where there are continuous flows of materials (for food, building, transport, clothing, etc.), including the waste arising from their use, of people (for work, for leisure, to support other people) and information (for controlling and monitoring transport, transferring money, ordering new supplies, using mobile phones, etc.), plus the energy services that provide heat, lighting and power for all the buildings, transport and equipment. These are just some of the services that underpin a modern, reasonably affluent lifestyle. We would find life very difficult to manage without them. This reliance on a complex web of infrastructure and services can make cities and their inhabitants surprisingly vulnerable to environmental hazards. Earthquakes, storms and floods regularly cause significant loss of life and economic losses to cities and towns, and can lead to evacuation. The subsequent disruption to 'normal' life can last for years.

There are two aspects of urban life that this example does not emphasise. A city is a place where there are considerable interactions with strangers – passing them in the street, sitting next to someone on a bus, talking to them in shops, ordering lunch – and these strangers are people with different jobs, interests, opinions, ages, and from varied backgrounds. All these interactions have to occur without causing too much social friction; city living is partly about doing this, for if it fails, the city becomes a place of danger. The second aspect not followed up is where the flows come from and go to. Clearly, people and materials move about both *within* the city (and who and what moves in and out of a particular district may well define much of its character), and to and from places *outside* the city. Cities rely and indeed thrive on connections and flows to the world outside, and the nature and strength of these are a usually a good guide to the size and character of the city as a whole.

Having looked at cities from two points of view, their historical development and the services they provide, one key attribute of a city begins to emerge: *cities are the centre of a network of connections*. The three diagrams in Figure 1.2 illustrate this idea for London by showing different aerial views of (a) the strength of connections of one of its networks, its roads, (b) the distribution of its population and (c) London lit up by night.

Its network of roads radiates from (or converges towards) the city centre, a pattern that is followed by the distribution of its population. At night its lights show that both population centres and roads are tightly connected. This pattern of communication links spreading out from the centre of cities is widespread and is sometimes described as the **hub and spoke** model. It shows that cities are at the centre of a network of connections of people and material and suggests that these connections intensify as you approach the centre. Not all towns or cities have this radial pattern. An alternative, commonly found in North American towns, for example in Los Angeles, but also in Milton Keynes in the UK, is to arrange city roads in a grid network, usually with one or more discernable centres that act as hubs or nodes. Whatever internal pattern is used, in a globalised world networks

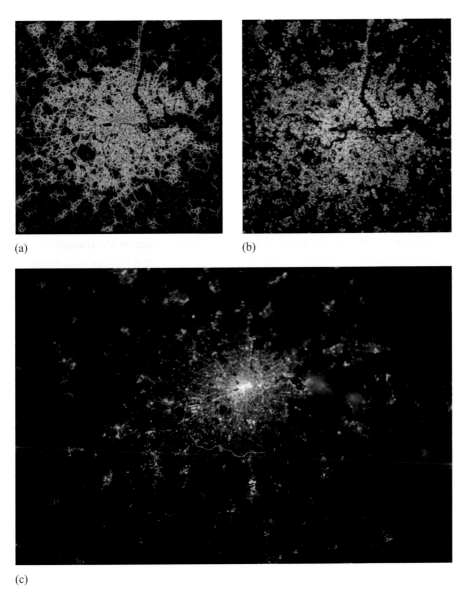

(a)

(b)

(c)

Figure 1.2 London connections: (a) the road network coloured by level of connectivity; (b) patterns of population density; (c) by night (more distant view)

spread from each city to all parts of the world. Everywhere is linked, town and countryside are connected, and the main difference between a town or village and a city is the level and intensity of the connections.

> Today we don't really live in a *civilisation*, but in a *mobilisation* – of natural resources, people and products. Cities are nodes from which mobility emanates: along roads, railway networks, aircraft routes and telephone lines. Cities also sprawl ever outwards along urban motorways and railway lines to their suburbs and shopping malls and beyond.
>
> *(Girardet, 1999, pp. 11, 12)*

This way of looking at cities does not explain why a particular city has developed or what is special about it, but an analysis of its flows and connections might well do so. It seems likely that all cities need a rich network of connections because without it they quickly decline. It also does not capture the internal richness of city life, its diversity, its different pressure groups and stakeholders, or its different attractions.

A final point follows from this description. Modern cities are above all *open* to the flow of people, ideas and materials. They may be built like fortresses but they do not behave like them. This means that the boundaries of a city can be difficult to define because its influence usually spreads far beyond any formal boundary. Indeed, different boundaries may be used for different purposes, depending on how the city is defined (or how its *system boundaries* are described; see Block 3, Part 1, Section 3.5). *Openness* makes cities more difficult to control or direct from above. Planners have often tried to direct people's behaviour or design towns, but both have a habit of developing in their own ways. Figure 1.3 illustrates three examples of

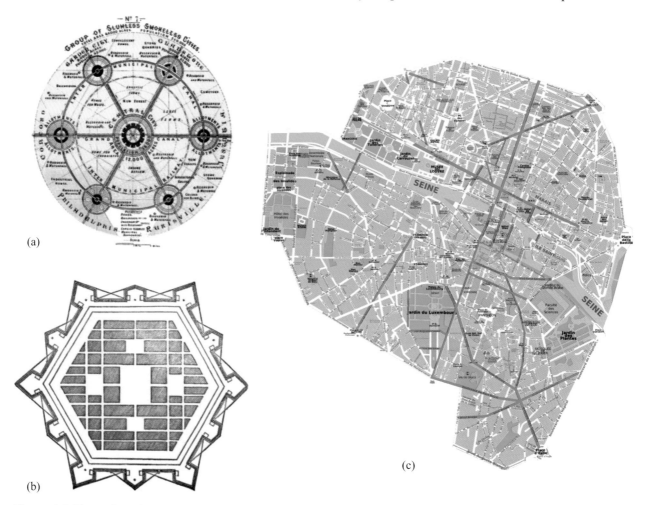

(a)

(b)

(c)

Figure 1.3 Examples of planned cities: (a) Howard's garden city of tomorrow; (b) idealised geometric city; (c) contemporary street map of Paris with remnants of Haussmann's road layout shown in red

planned cities. The first two contain clear geometric shapes and designs and are quite unlike the messy, tangled structures of London apparent in Figure 1.2. Very few real cities turn out quite as neatly as the original conceptions shown here. Many appear to grow fairly haphazardly in response to conflicting pressures and demands, or consist of a series of designs or modifications to existing patterns, as shown for example in Figure 1.3(c) by Haussmann's 1860 plans for the renewal of Paris, which included both radial and grid patterns.

Jonathan Raban and Walter Benjamin are two social scientists who have attempted to describe and explain cities by focusing on their people rather than the infrastructure. They take the view that the great wealth of cities resides not in their buildings and infrastructure but in the knowledge and creativity of their people. Openness, for them, is the source of both strengths and weaknesses, as this quote from Melville explains:

> Openness, what Raban calls 'soft' and Walter Benjamin 'porous', implies vulnerability – it's the price we pay for our privilege. But it is also – like flexibility as opposed to rigidity – a great strength. This openness resides not in the infrastructure, the buildings or the great parks, the museums, the office blocks. Nor in the strategies of government, police or the London Assembly, but in the tactics of the people who use it, who make the city by traversing it.

> *(Melville, 2006)*

1.1.3   Can cities be sustainable?

Cities have usually been created to last, and the majority have done exactly that, growing, evolving and reinventing themselves as circumstances change. As earlier sections have pointed out, successful cities are dynamic places:

- they rely and indeed thrive on connections and flows to the world outside
- they are above all *open* to the flow of people, ideas and materials.

To thrive, cities have had to meet the economic and social aspirations of their populations and no doubt satisfy the political ambitions of their leaders. But longevity does not mean that they have been organised on sustainable principles; *environmental* concerns have rarely been a high priority. Indeed, many would say that cities typify unsustainable ways of living. They import large amounts of materials and energy, partly to produce goods for other cities and partly for direct consumption or to maintain the city infrastructure. They send out produced goods and a variety of waste products. In an ecological sense cities are decidedly not sustainable because they rely on large numbers of other people and on production from large areas of land and water to service and feed them and to remove their waste products. They have large and increasing environmental impacts. Thus the citizens of London, or any rich city today, are using products from China and the Amazon; their desire for all kinds of food and consumer goods to be available every day of the year is a major reason why tropical forests are being logged and burned, and their waste products contribute to the warming of the Arctic and the melting of its ice. They also rely on the labour of a great many poor people for their goods and services and often contain within their boundaries large disparities of wealth. Cities have always relied on the labour of the poor for their smooth functioning. This is a significant part of the reason why cities are very vulnerable to environmental hazards, for example the flooding of New Orleans in 2005. It is almost always the poorer populations that suffer most.

This does not necessarily mean that urbanisation and living in cities is the main cause of the world's environmental problems. It is simply more visible because cities contain the greatest concentrations of people. But concentration or intensity of flows are not necessarily a disadvantage; they can lead to more efficient ways of providing goods and services. For example, in parts of southern England the environmental impact of individuals living in the regions surrounding its main cities can be high as or higher than that of city dwellers (WWF, 2006). Some aspects of urban life, for example living more closely together, living in flats or apartments rather than detached houses and using public transport, can lead to considerable reductions in energy consumption for heating and transport compared with living in the country or in a village.

1.1.4   Rethinking the city

Is it possible to re-imagine a city that can meet today's environmental concerns, while not forgetting the social needs of its population or stifling economic dynamism, the requirements of openness and of maintaining rich connections to the rest of the world? What does it mean to look at a city from an environmental standpoint? It means asking questions like:

- What are the global and local environmental impacts of a city, and how significant are they?
- How vulnerable are cities to environmental pressures or threats, like floods or pollution?
- What are the environmental issues or concerns of its inhabitants?
- What does a sustainable city mean?

These questions suggest that both the city infrastructure and the needs of its people should be considered. Decisions about infrastructure are significant because it will be in place for many decades, and once it has been built it tends to lock a city into certain forms of transport and use of materials; a road layout or a railway system are examples of this. People are important because it is we who are ultimately going to find the solutions to problems and if we don't like what has been planned we will try to find alternatives or stop it happening. If we don't like the home being offered we will reject it or change it to suit our needs. However, designing and building new infrastructure usually has to be planned city-wide rather than left to individuals. Finding a suitable process of consultation and participation that satisfies and involves all who might be affected is by no means easy.

One way of thinking about cities that involves both people and the idea of networks and connections is to view them either as growing organisms or as ecosystems. This should not be taken too literally, but if used as a metaphor for a complicated system it can help remind decision makers that the influence of people and communities in shaping their urban environment is never straightforward. This approach also has the advantage of helping to explain material flows into and out of cities and pointing to how they might be modified. It leads naturally to the idea that a city has an environmental 'footprint' that can be measured in various ways – ecological and carbon footprints have been discussed in earlier blocks. This, in turn, can help to answer questions about the environmental impact of cities and whether their current consumption patterns can be sustained.

Human societies, though strongly influenced by ecological restraints, have always had the ability to adapt to changing circumstances. This can be both a strength and a weakness. It has allowed us to exploit the Earth's resources for our own ends while largely ignoring, until recently, their environmental impact. Because cities concentrate and direct the flows of materials that they use, consume and then throw away, they have always had environmental impacts on their surroundings. This is not just a modern problem, but as material flows have increased environmental impacts have become more widespread. The challenge now is to learn to soften our impact, particularly in cities, while still leading fulfilling lives and meeting our material and social needs. This means rethinking cities from top to bottom while viewing them and assessing them from an environmental standpoint.

There are, perhaps, three ways of imagining changed cities. One is to confront problems as they arise and to adapt the city to meet new threats or opportunities. This is the route of organic growth and adaptation that most cities have followed.

Another is to start completely from scratch and design a new city based on new environmental principles, as illustrated by Howard's garden city in Figure 1.3 – what today is often called an eco-city. As mentioned in Section 1.1.2, cities often develop in unexpected directions, or plans prove to be unworkable, so modern planners and designers spend a lot of effort trying to anticipate all possible problems. Two examples of eco-cities are introduced in Part 3 of this block, and you can make up your own mind to what extent they could be called sustainable, and whether this is a viable blueprint for future cities.

There is a third way, one that is gaining momentum. Local communities are showing their openness to change by taking their own initiatives in a great variety of ways – in their homes, their street, their school, their businesses, their village or town, including the Transition Town initiatives. They are making positive use of our boundless creativity to adapt to changing circumstances. Spend a few minutes thinking about how you might do this in your community.

Activity 1.4   Looking at your town in a new light

Take a moment to reflect on how you might change *one* aspect of your village, town or city to reduce its environmental impact. What problems might this raise?

Discussion

I found this activity quite challenging. I live in a poorer city neighbourhood where environmental issues are not high on the agenda, though like many other local authorities recycling has recently been introduced, with a fair degree of success. What I observe is that overall compliance is good, and most people in my street are happy to adapt to the new ways and some are pleased to be doing their 'bit' for the environment. Several leaflets accompanied this initiative, explaining what needed to be done and how the local authority would be doing its 'bit', but after a year everything just became routine. What I would like to see is some way of encouraging individuals and households to feel good about what they are doing by explaining how they are contributing, and to find ways to continue to improve what is being done by involving them more. This would involve more education and feedback and be costly in terms of time. It might also set some people against the scheme if they were only grudging supporters. The local authority and the private firm that carries out the scheme may be reluctant to change what they are doing without incentives. It would need a lot of energy and careful planning and consultation, and would probably have to rely on existing community organisations.

Clearly your own answer will depend on your circumstances and your interests. It is quite possible that answering this activity got you thinking about what a sustainable initiative means. What would a sustainable project, or better still a sustainable city, look like? Richard Rogers, the UK architect and urban planner, describes his vision of a sustainable city and reminds us that if we are to re-imagine a successful city we need to consider its economic dynamism and its attractions for all of its population, as well as its environmental credentials.

The sustainable city is:

A Just City, where justice, food, shelter, education, health and hope are fairly distributed

A Beautiful City, where art, architecture, and landscape spark the imagination and move the spirit

A Creative City, where open-mindedness and experimentation mobilise the full potential of its human resources and allows fast response to change

An Ecological City, which minimises its ecological impact, where landscape and built form are balanced and where buildings and infrastructures are safe and resource efficient

A City of Easy Contact and Mobility, where information is exchanged both face to face and electronically

A Compact and Polycentric City, which protects the countryside, focuses and integrates the communities within neighbourhoods and maximises proximity

A Diverse City, where a broad range of overlapping activities create animation, inspiration and foster a vital public life.

(Rogers, 1998)

Some of the aspects of a sustainable city that Rogers suggests – a creative city, a city of easy contact and mobility, a diverse city – have been touched on in this section. Others will be mentioned elsewhere in Block 6. The aim of re-imagining cities is to find ways – any ways – of making cities and city living sustainable and is the key question for Block 6.

Part 1 now turns to London's past to explore in depth two examples of how nineteenth-century London, its political leaders, scientists and engineers, found ways to adapt to pressing environmental threats, and how this affected Londoners' lives and even the way they thought about their homes. Bazalgette's solution to the 'Great Stink', which you will read about shortly, inspired Haussmann to submit his plans for the redesign of Paris. The intention of Part 1 is to use these examples to inform those who today are trying to make cities more sustainable.

Summary of Section 1

Cities and other urban areas are built environments where large numbers of people live, work and relax. Early cities relied on a strong state as well as food, water and communications. Modern cities are the centre of networks of connections and have to be open to flows of people, materials, energy services, to information and ideas, and they have large environmental impacts. Cities can also be viewed as growing organisms or ecosystems.

2 A brief look at London past

The city of London grew up beside the River Thames in Roman times. It was strategically located at the lowest convenient crossing place of the river, London Bridge. To the south-east the main road, Watling Street, ran to Canterbury and Dover and across the Channel to the roads to Rome. To the north roads ran to St Albans and the rest of England (see Figure 1.4).

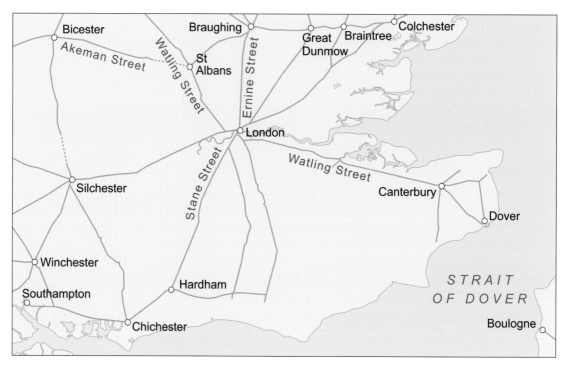

Figure 1.4 Roman London's strategic location

The Roman city itself was located on the high ground of the current City of London (the 'square mile') and St Paul's Cathedral. The river was wide enough to allow seagoing ships to be turned and unloaded. The city thrived and by AD140 had a population of about 50 000. It was one of the major cities of the Roman Empire. The twin city of Westminster grew up on an island in the marshes two miles further upstream. When the Romans left in the fourth century London fell on hard times, but it was sufficiently important for William the Conqueror to have himself crowned King of England at Westminster in 1066. Westminster remained the seat of the government for most of the following millennium. Its companion city, London, has always been granted special privileges by the monarch; for example, London was not surveyed for William's Domesday Book.

London only returned to its Roman size in about the fourteenth century but continued to grow. Despite the long journey up the winding Thames from the sea, the port of London thrived. It was becoming the trading port for a whole British Empire. By 1700 London's population was over half a million. The physical size of London was constrained by how far people were prepared to walk every day from their home to work. Housing densities were very high and the streets were choked with people and horses. In 1800 nearly a million people were packed into an area of barely 10 square miles (see Figure 1.5). Since road transport was relatively difficult, particularly in winter, fresh food was grown locally or brought by boat from farms along the Thames.

The introduction of railways in the 1830s and the provision of cheap workmen's trains allowed a rapid expansion of the city into the surrounding fields. This created an enormous area of commuter suburbia

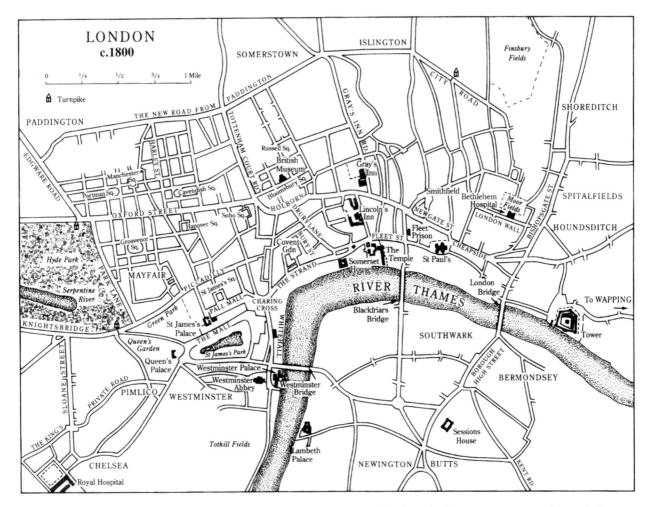

Figure 1.5 London at the beginning of the nineteenth century. At this time the Thames was crossed by only three bridges: Westminster Bridge, Blackfriars Bridge and London Bridge. The river downstream of London Bridge would have been full of ships waiting to unload at the quays on either side of the river *(Source: Ackroyd, 2000)*

(see Figure 1.6), setting the pattern for the expansion of many other cities. When in 1889 the London County Council was set up it administered an area of nearly 120 square miles and 5.5 million people.

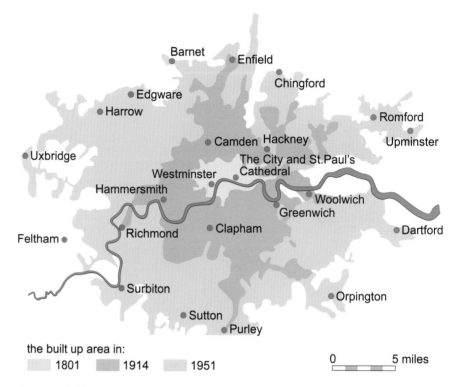

Figure 1.6 The growth of London 1801–1951 *(Source: adapted from White, 1963)*

By the mid-nineteenth century Britain was the richest country in Europe and London was the largest city in the world. It was a trading port, a manufacturing centre and a centre of finance and insurance. It produced about one-sixth of the country's GDP.

For the more privileged, London was a city of bright lights and shops filled with consumer goods (Figure 1.7).

The rich and the middle class could afford to move out to the suburbs. The poor remained trapped in slums in inner London, such as those portrayed by the engraver Gustav Doré in 1872 (Figure 1.8).

While London offered the benefits of modern urban living to many, the disbenefits of pollution, particularly those of sewage and smoke, also had to be dealt with.

Figure 1.7 Shopping in the Brompton Road in 1895. Note the large gas display lights outside the shops (they generated too much heat to put inside)

Figure 1.8 *Over London by Rail*, the dirt and squalor of London slums as depicted in an 1872 engraving by Gustav Doré

SAQ 1.1   The siting of Roman London

Why did the Romans choose to build London where they did?

Summary of Section 2

In this section I have looked briefly at the reasons for the current location of London and at its growth, particularly during the nineteenth century.

3 The Great Stink of 1858

The original units of tons, feet and cubic yards have been retained here. Note that 1 ton = 1.016 tonnes, 1 foot = 0.305 m and 1 cubic yard = 0.76 m³

3.1 'The Thames is now made a great cesspool'

By 1840 London's population had reached two million. It had doubled since the beginning of the century. The Great Exhibition held in Hyde Park in 1851 was intended as a trade fair to celebrate Britain's industrial success, but it also became an enormous tourist attraction for ordinary people. Six million people visited it. London was *the* city to go to.

But it had a worsening sewage problem. At that time, as it had been for centuries, most of London's sewage waste was recycled. Individual houses had cesspools (though often these were actually just the cellars); there were an estimated 200 000 in London in 1810. The solid waste or 'night-soil' was collected from these by well-paid 'nightmen' (they were only allowed to work at night) who transported it to the market gardens surrounding the city. Here it was sold as fertiliser. The waste water either seeped into the ground or flowed through the streets into the old natural rivers, which had become public sewers. These all eventually flowed out into the River Thames.

Two factors made the situation worse. The first was the continuing expansion of the built-up area of the city. This meant that the night-soil had to be transported further and further (by horse and cart) to reach the fields.

The second was the development of the flush toilet or water closet (see Figure 1.9). Although invented in Elizabethan times, it was redesigned in a form suitable for mass production by Joseph Bramah in 1778. The Great Exhibition itself promoted their use. An enterprising manufacturer called George Jennings installed them for public use and an estimated 827 000 people used them, no doubt many experiencing their use for the first time.

The use of water closets (WCs) required large amounts of water; indeed, they were only practicable where piped water was available. Their popularity increased sales of water by the private water companies and also the overall flow through the existing sewers. This overwhelmed the storage capacity of the traditional cesspools and added a tide of solid waste into the sewers. Prior to 1815 it had been illegal to connect cesspools to the public drains, but this prohibition was lifted. The existing sewers were, in a

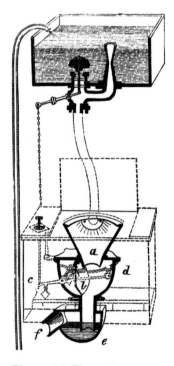

Figure 1.9 The water closet became increasingly popular in the first half of the nineteenth century. This shows a rather complicated version of the 1850s

piecemeal fashion, enlarged and improved, but this just shifted the basic problem. As the contractor Thomas Cubitt put it in 1840:

> Fifty years ago nearly all London had every house cleansed into a large cesspool … Now sewers having been very much improved, scarcely any person thinks of making a cesspool, but it is carried off at once into the river. It would be a great improvement if that could be carried off independently of the town, but the Thames is now made a great cesspool instead of each person having one of his own.
>
> *(Quoted in Halliday, 1999)*

3.2   London's water supply

The city also had a water supply problem. Some came from shallow wells within the city and was delivered by the bucketful. More prosperous areas had piped water provided by private water companies from springs in the hills around London, or from the Thames itself. Some companies took their water right in the centre of the city, while others had water intakes further upstream. In itself, this was no guarantee of clean water. The tidal nature of the Thames meant that sewage discharged in the city centre at low tide might be carried quite a distance upstream before starting its journey to the sea.

The overall deterioration of the quality of Thames river water had been reflected in the number of fish caught. Local salmon were once common and were sold in London markets. As late as 1816, fourteen salmon had been caught at Taplow, about 20 miles west of London. By 1820, no catches of salmon were recorded at all. It would be over 150 years before they started to return.

SAQ 1.2   The water closet – an invention with problems

What benefits did the increased use of WCs bring and what problems did it create? Who benefited and who suffered as a result?

3.3   Cholera arrives

In 1831, during a global outbreak of the disease, cholera arrived in Britain. It had originated in India but had spread right across Europe. The main symptom is acute diarrhoea, which drains the body of nutrients and fluids. This leads to dehydration, kidney failure and death, often within only a few hours of the onset of the disease. The 1831 outbreak killed over 6000 people in London. Further outbreaks in 1848–9 and 1853–4 killed another 25 000 Londoners.

At the time, the cause of the disease was a mystery and the efforts of doctors to enforce quarantines were met with public hostility. There were riots in Liverpool in 1832. However, these were not as serious as those that had taken place in St Petersburg in Russia, which had had to be put down by the army.

The link between the disease and the contamination of drinking water by human sewage was suspected by some, such as Dr John Snow (see Box 1.1). The dominant opinion was the *'miasmatic theory'*, which held that disease was spread by smells and 'foul air'.

Box 1.1   Dr John Snow and the miasmatic theory

Figure 1.10 Dr John Snow

Dr John Snow had a successful medical practice in Soho in central London and was a pioneer in the use of anaesthetics. In his early career he had observed the effects of the 1831 cholera epidemic on miners in Newcastle. In 1849 he published a paper suggesting that the mechanism for the spread of the disease was drinking water that had been contaminated with infected sewage. When the London outbreak of 1854 occurred he was able to carry out what would now be called an 'epidemiological investigation' into the outbreak at close quarters. He noticed the high incidence of cholera among people who drew water from a shallow well in Broad Street (now called Broadwick Street) and drew up a map carefully plotting the disease deaths (see Figure 1.11).

With the aid of a local vicar, he carried out a detailed investigation that included interviewing the survivors. He showed that the outbreak had started with the water used to wash the nappies of a sick baby being thrown into a sewer only a few feet from the well. The contamination continued as the rest of the family sickened and died. His arguments were sufficient to persuade the local parish council to remove the handle from the pump, but not before 96 people living in Broad Street alone had died in the space of under two weeks.

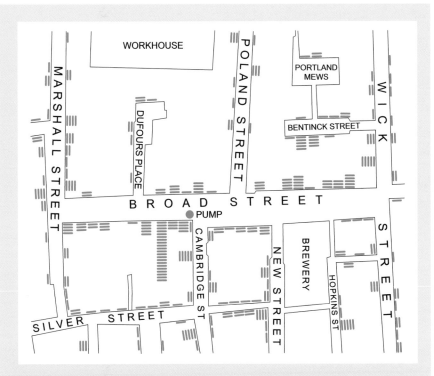

Figure 1.11 Dr John Snow's 'Ghost map'. Each red line represents a cholera death. The water pump in Broad Street was suspiciously located at the centre of the outbreak *(Source: redrawn from Johnson, 2006)*

However, the conventional 'miasmatic theory' had influential supporters including public health campaigner Edwin Chadwick (see Box 1.2), who in 1846 told a Parliamentary Committee: 'All smell is, if it be intense, immediate acute disease.' Another was Florence Nightingale, best known for her reports on conditions in the Crimean War.

The battle raged on to the end of the nineteenth century as scientists developed the germ theory of disease. The German bacteriologist Robert Koch identified the cholera bacillus in India in 1883 and showed that it was conveyed in polluted water, as Snow had suggested. Koch was eventually awarded the Nobel Prize for Medicine in 1905.

3.4 Who was responsible for London's public health?

One initial problem was that of jurisdiction. Who was actually responsible for London as a whole? The built-up area of London had spread out from the original Roman city, around St Paul's Cathedral, into the surrounding fields and villages. The aldermen of the City of London were jealous of their traditional privileges. Around them about two million people were governed by the local vestries, or councils, of a range of parishes, precincts and liberties. In some the vestrymen were elected, in others they were appointed by 'principal inhabitants'.

In 1855 *The Times* commented:

> There is no such place as London at all. [… It is] rent into an infinity of divisions, districts and areas […] Within the Metropolitan limits the local administration is carried on by no fewer than three hundred different bodies, deriving powers from about two hundred and fifty local Acts.

(Quoted in Halliday, 1999)

Dealing with the problems of sewage and public health raised the need for a larger, more central authority but created conflict with the existing fragmented 'local government'. It would, as Snow put it in 1849, need 'doing away with that form of liberty to which some communities cling, the sacred power to poison to death not only themselves but their neighbours'.

The outspoken campaigner Edwin Chadwick was of a similar opinion:

> The chief remedies consist in applications of the science of engineering, of which the medical men know nothing; and to gain powers for their applications, and to deal with local rights which stand in the way of practical improvements, some jurisprudence is necessary, of which engineers know nothing.

(Quoted in Halliday, 1999)

Box 1.2   Edwin Chadwick

Figure 1.12 Edwin Chadwick

Born in 1800, Edwin Chadwick was a vigorous campaigner for social reform but he had an extraordinary ability to upset his co-workers. He believed that poor social conditions led to disease and should be dealt with by strong government authorities. He was particularly enthusiastic about gathering detailed statistics, which gave his reports to Parliament considerable weight, but often created great resentment elsewhere. He turned to sanitary reform in the 1840s and in 1848 became a member of the Metropolitan Sewers Commission. He raised so much antagonism that in 1849 he was barred from it.

He was a firm believer in the 'miasmatic theory' of disease and continued to campaign for the agricultural use of sewage sludge into the 1870s. He was knighted in 1889 and died the following year.

The establishment of London-wide authorities provoked heated arguments, with Chadwick arguing for a central body to control both water and sewage. This did not make him popular with the water companies. At the other extreme, a barrister by the name of J. Toulmin Smith preached a libertarian view, promoting his 'Anti-Centralisation Union' and arguing that sewers were an unnecessary expense.

A precedent for London-wide organisations was set in 1829 when the Metropolitan Police Force was created. This recognised the existence of a London 'metropolis' with defined boundaries. However, its jurisdiction did not include the City of London which, to this day, has its own separate police force.

In 1848 the government established a Metropolitan Commission of Sewers to coordinate work carried out by the vestries. It had a radius of jurisdiction of twelve miles from St Paul's Cathedral, but did not include the City of London. The Act of Parliament that set it up also now insisted that all new buildings should have a WC and that it should be connected to a public sewer if there was one within 100 feet. Alternative earth or ash closets were also permitted.

Sadly, the powers of the Commission were initially not even adequate to order a full detailed Ordnance Survey map to be made of London's sewers and house drains (requested at a scale of 10 feet to the mile!). It took until 1858 to complete, but was an essential task.

Activity 1.5   Who is responsible for your sewage?

Who do you think should be responsible for your sewage? Is it a matter for the individual householder, the local council or some city-wide authority?

Discussion
Today we would accept that urban sewage should be collected and 'treated'. This requires some organisation of an appropriate scale, but this could be seen as an agent of the 'interfering nanny state'.

For J. Toulmin Smith any more government was a 'bad thing'. The urban household should look after its own sewage (and presumably pay a night-soil man to take it away). At the other extreme, Edwin Chadwick thought it required 'government action'. The government decided on a city-wide approach, setting up the Metropolitan Commission of Sewers with a defined radius of action.

3.5   No filth in the sewers – all in the river!

Chadwick advocated that the Commission's policy should be: 'the complete drainage and purification of the dwelling house, next of the street and lastly of the river'. *The Times* summarised this as 'no filth in the sewers, all in the river'. The engineers even documented exactly how much filth had been dumped into the river. For example: 80,000 cubic yards from September 1848 to February 1849 (Halliday, 1999).

In 1849 the Commission started looking into the possibilities of separating the sewage sludge for use as fertiliser. The arguments over rival schemes became so acrimonious that Chadwick, who had done so much campaigning to set up the Commission, was barred from it. The Commission then issued a general invitation to engineers to submit proposals for dealing with London's sewage.

At this point an engineer named Joseph Bazalgette (see Box 1.3) was hired. He was given the task of analysing the 137 plans submitted to the Commission. These included:

schemes for organised night-soil collection

schemes for deodorising the sewage before discharging it into the Thames

a system of intercepting tunnels next to the Thames to carry the sewage further downstream.

By 1850 it was concluded that none of them were completely satisfactory.

Box 1.3   Joseph Bazalgette

Figure 1.13 Joseph Bazalgette in about 1865

Bazalgette was born in Enfield in 1819 and in his early career worked as an engineer on land drainage in Northern Ireland. In 1842 he set up his own civil engineering practice on London, working on railways, ship canals and other engineering projects. His health gave way through overwork in 1847 and he had to take a year off in the country. In 1849 he was appointed Assistant Surveyor to the Metropolitan Commission of Sewers and in 1856 he became chief engineer for the Metropolitan Board of Works. He was knighted in 1874 and retired in 1889, dying in Wimbledon two years later.

3.6   The press campaign

The press was in no doubt that something would have to be done about the twin problems of sewage contamination of the Thames and its use as drinking water. There was heated discussion in *The Times* newspaper and satirical cartoons in the weekly magazine *Punch* (see Figure 1.14).

(a)   (b)

Figure 1.14 (a) An 1850 *Punch* cartoon of 'The Wonders of a London Water Drop'; (b) 'Michael Faraday presenting his card to Father Thames', *Punch*, July 1855

In July 1855 the celebrated scientist Michael Faraday wrote to *The Times*. He described how he had taken a steamboat ride on the Thames and tested the clarity of the water by dropping pieces of white card into it. They rapidly disappeared before they had 'sunk an inch' into the 'opaque, pale brown fluid'. He continued: 'The smell was very bad and common to the whole of the water. […] If we neglect this subject, we cannot expect to do so with impunity, nor ought we to be surprised if, ere many years are over, a hot season gives us sad proof of the folly of our carelessness' (Quoted in Halliday, 1999).

3.7   The Metropolitan Board of Works

Also in 1855 the Metropolitan Local Management Bill was put through Parliament. This rather cautious bill attempted to centralise some aspects of the administration of London. It created the Metropolitan Board of Works, one of whose duties was to 'make such sewers and works as they may think necessary for preventing all and any part of the sewage of the Metropolis from flowing into the River Thames in or near the Metropolis' (Quoted in Halliday, 1999). These ambitious words were later to prove a considerable stumbling block.

Joseph Bazalgette was appointed chief engineer for the Board. He took his duties very seriously and shortly produced a detailed plan for a scheme of intercepting sewers (see Figure 1.15). These would collect the sewage from the existing sewers either as it flowed into the Thames or further inland. On the north bank it would be carried eastwards as far as Beckton, eight miles east of St Paul's Cathedral, to be stored and then discharged on the outgoing tide. On the south bank the sewage would flow as far as Crossness, two miles further downstream, where the same would happen. Most of the scheme was very carefully designed to flow by gravity, but at key points all of the sewage would have to be pumped to a higher level using enormous steam pumps.

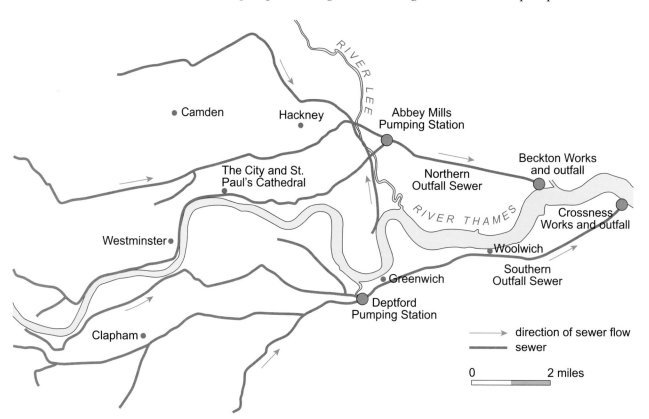

Figure 1.15 Bazalgette's system of intercepting sewers (*Source: adapted from Halliday, 1999*)

There then followed two years of arguments, mainly with the Chief Commissioner of Works, the MP Benjamin Hall, who was also responsible for completing the construction of the Houses of Parliament ('Big Ben' is named after him). There were many questions:

> Did Bazalgette's scheme satisfy the requirements of the 1855 Act in preventing 'all and any part of the sewage of the Metropolis from flowing into the River Thames in or near the Metropolis'? Surely 10 miles was 'near' the metropolis. In 1857 Hall commissioned a rival proposal which suggested carrying it a further 15 miles closer to the sea to Mucking Creek, near Canvey Island.

Would it be value for money? Bazalgette's initial estimates were that his scheme would cost almost £2.5 million (about £250 million in today's money). The Mucking Creek scheme would cost twice as much.

If it was the smell that caused disease, shouldn't the sewage be deodorised?

Could the sewage sludge be sold for fertiliser? At the time British farmers were willing to pay £8–10 a ton for 'guano', dried concentrated bird droppings, imported all the way from the Pacific coast of South America. One (optimistic) estimate suggested that 125 000 tons of dry manure per year could be recovered from London sewage and sold at a profit of £190 000. Taken over a decade or more, this potential income could almost pay for the whole sewage scheme.

3.8   The 'Great Stink' forces action

The weather of the first two weeks of June 1858 was exceptionally hot, and nowhere was it more unpleasant than in the brand new Houses of Parliament. Construction had started in 1840 following a disastrous fire which had destroyed most of the old Palace of Westminster in 1834. The new building (Figure 1.16) was partly built on land reclaimed from the Thames. The design was lavish. It was originally estimated to cost about £700 000 but ended up costing three times as much. It used the latest theories of natural ventilation, drawing 'fresh' air from the terrace overlooking the Thames and exhausting stale air through the pinnacles on the roof.

Figure 1.16 The Houses of Parliament today. These were almost complete in 1858 and could hardly have been closer to the Thames

The location and timing could not have been worse. By the summer of 1858 the building was almost complete (and the money spent). The trouble was that it threatened to be unusable.

The Times relished the irony of the situation, commenting on 18 June 1858:

> What a pity [it is] that the thermometer fell ten degrees yesterday. Parliament was all but compelled to legislate upon the great London nuisance by the force of sheer stench. The intense heat had driven our legislators from those portions of their buildings which overlook the river. A few members, bent upon investigating the matter to its very depth, ventured into the library, but they were instantaneously driven to retreat, each man with a handkerchief to his nose. We are heartily glad of it.

(Quoted in Halliday, 1999)

SAQ 1.3   The dreadful smell in the library

Why might MPs venturing into the library of the Houses of Parliament have been particularly worried about the smell?

The 'force of stench' did indeed force the government to act. On 15 July Benjamin Disraeli, as Leader of the House of Commons, introduced a new bill in Parliament, the Metropolis Local Management Amendment Bill. One key element was to reword the 1855 Act so that the sewage system would be for 'preventing as far as may be practicable, the sewage of the Metropolis from passing into the River Thames within the Metropolis' (Quoted in Halliday, 1999).

These vital words, 'as far as may be practicable', meant that, at a stroke, Bazalgette's scheme could be used rather than the Mucking Creek one, and £2.5 million saved.

Today, this approach would be described as using the Best Available Technology Not Entailing Excessive Cost, or *BATNEEC*.

The bill also gave the Metropolitan Board of Works power to borrow £3 million, guaranteed by the Treasury, to be repaid over 40 years by the ratepayers of London.

On 21 July, before the actual debate began, *The Times* attacked the past dithering:

> This is a case where the fool's argument that 'something must be done' is applicable […] The actions of the [Metropolitan] Board were crippled in two most important respects. It had no money and it had no power […] if we wait for a concurrence of opinions on this subject, we shall never stick a spade in the ground. […] The stench of June was only the last ounce of our burden. That hot fortnight did for the sanitary administration of the Metropolis what the Bengal mutinies did for the administration of India.

(Quoted in Halliday, 1999)

The bill was debated for three days and became law on 2 August. Only 18 days after the bill had been introduced and two months after the 'Great Stink' the required Act of Parliament was put in place for Bazalgette to start work.

3.9   Construction begins

The scheme was an extraordinary feat of engineering. Bazalgette replaced 165 miles of old sewers as well as constructing 1100 miles of new ones. It required 82 miles of intercepting sewers laid to a minimum fall of 2 feet per mile.

These had to connect with existing ones and then be built through crowded streets, over and under existing canals and railways. Provision had to be made to cope with heavy rainfall while keeping an adequate flow in the sewers in dry weather.

Fifty-two acres of land were reclaimed from the Thames. The squalid riverfront of the Strand was turned into the Victoria Embankment. This housed both the intercepting sewer and the new District Underground Railway. And, thanks to the intervention of a certain W. H. Smith, bookstall entrepreneur, it was kept as open space.

The construction consumed 318 million bricks (see Figure 1.17) and demand was such that it forced up the price of them in London by about 50%. The need for more bricklayers meant that wages had to be increased from 5 shillings (25 pence) per day to 6 shillings (30 pence) or more. It consumed nearly a million cubic yards of concrete. A special mill was built at Crossness to produce this, together with a railway to distribute it.

Figure 1.17 Bricklayers working on the Northern Outfall Sewer in 1859

The project made pioneering use of Portland cement, which was water resistant, rather than conventional lime mortar. Because its manufacturing process was so new, Bazalgette insisted on a draconian regime of quality control, with every batch being tested before it was used.

It required the excavation of 3.5 million cubic yards of earth. This was all done by hand – there were no mechanical diggers at the time. It also required enormous steam engines to pump the sewage. Those installed at Deptford in 1864 were at the time the largest ever built.

Needless to say, the project went over budget and in 1863 a further £1.2 million had to be borrowed, bringing the bill to over £4 million.

This was truly a prestige scheme. Although most of it was underground, the buildings that did show, such as the pumping stations, were lavishly decorated, even inside. The southern drainage scheme was completed in 1865 and the northern one in 1868. The pumping stations were opened by royalty and even the sewage pumps were named after members of the royal family (see Figure 1.18).

(a)

(c)

(b)

Figure 1.18   (a) The Crossness pumping station at the time of its opening in 1865; (b) the Prince of Wales opening the steam sewage pump at Crossness, named after him, in 1865; (c) 'The Prince Consort' sewage pump at Crossness as restored to its original brilliant colours in 2007

3.10　Did it work?

There was a further outbreak of cholera in east London in 1866. Although the southern half of Bazalgette's scheme was in operation by this time, the northern section was not. There were nearly 4000 deaths over two months in an area served by the East London Water Company. The outbreak was traced to infected sewage in the tidal river Lea (also spelt Lee), a tributary of the Thames, seeping into one of the water company's reservoirs. This was good support for Snow's theories but the water companies rushed to employ expert witnesses and lawyers to plead in court how pure their water was. As the statistician William Farr commented, it was a lot easier to blame disease on the air and the 'miasmatic theory' since:

> As the air of London is not supplied like water to its inhabitants by companies the air has had the worst of it both before Parliamentary Committees and Royal Commissions. For air no scientific witnesses have been retained, no learned counsel has pleaded …

(Quoted in Halliday, 1999)

This outbreak was the last in London, and in 1892, when an epidemic reached Hamburg, killing 8600 people, London was spared completely.

Box 1.4 shows the progress of improvements to London's sewers.

Box 1.4　Timeline: improving London's sewers	
1815	House cesspools permitted to be connected to public sewers for the first time
1820	Salmon disappear from the Thames
1831	Cholera reaches Britain; 40 000 Londoners die in four epidemics
1855	Michael Faraday writes to *The Times* complaining about the filthy Thames
1856	Metropolitan Board of Works created, with Bazalgette as chief engineer
1856–8	Bazalgette and Benjamin Hall argue about the suitability of the drainage system
1858	The Great Stink. Parliament grants Bazalgette the authority and money required to implement his system
1865	Southern drainage completed
1866	The final cholera epidemic in east London
1867	Northern drainage completed
1891	Cholera strikes Hamburg; London unaffected.

Activity 1.6   A heated parliamentary debate

In July 1858 Parliament furiously debated the need to spend £3 million on a new sewage system for London. It became law only 18 days later. Consider the issues that they would have debated:

1　How well understood was the science of diseases like cholera?

2　What might happen if there was a serious cholera epidemic?

3　Was it the role of the national government to tell individual households what to do with their sewage?

4　The previous 1855 Act had said that London's sewage should not be put in the Thames at all 'near the Metropolis'. This new bill now said that this only applied 'as far as may be practicable'. Shouldn't the government be insisting on doing things properly?

5　How important was the influence of the press?

Discussion

1　The science of diseases like cholera was not well understood at all in 1858. Influential people like Florence Nightingale believed in the 'miasmatic theory' and it would take another 40 years for the germ theory of disease to be accepted.

2　In the cholera outbreak of 1854, over 600 people died in London and a total of 23 000 people had died in Britain. In 1832 there had been riots in Liverpool when doctors tried to enforce quarantines. In Russia the rioting had been so bad that the army had to be brought in.

3　Although those like Chadwick campaigned for strong government action to deal with social issues, there were plenty like J. Toulmin Smith who believed in the freedom of the individual. Dr Snow felt that it was a matter of 'doing away with that form of liberty to which some communities cling, the sacred power to poison to death not only themselves but their neighbours'.

4　Parliament had to 'do something' (and be seen to do it). Had the 'force of stench' not been so immediate, Parliament might have asked Benjamin Hall to commission more studies. What was on offer was Bazalgette's scheme costed at £2.5 million and the Mucking Creek scheme at £5 million. They chose the cheaper of the two options, the BATNEEC approach, the Best Available Technology Not Entailing Excessive Cost.

5　*The Times* had been a focus for discussion by important scientists like Michael Faraday. The press had no doubt that the dithering had to stop! Woe betide any politician who wanted further delay!

3.11   Was it a long-term solution?

As an investment in urban infrastructure, Bazalgette's sewers must be rated as extremely good value for money. Given that the GDP of London was about £200 million per year at the time, £4 million spent on a sewage system was not that expensive. The capital cost was paid off after 40 years, but the sewers are still in use today. Even many of the steam pumps, after some efficiency improvements, worked on into the 1950s.

After the scheme was put into full operation in 1868, the London press had nothing but praise. The streets and the Thames in central London were certainly sweeter smelling. Bazalgette himself publicised accounts of fish actually being caught at Westminster.

However, a steady tide of complaints now came from further downstream. One particularly nasty incident in 1878 focused attention on the state of the river. The pleasure steamer *Princess Alice* collided with a freighter and sank near the outfalls, with the loss of 600 lives. There were suggestions that many of the dead had been poisoned by the river water rather than simply drowning.

In 1882 a group of MPs formed the 'General Committee of the Protection of the Lower Thames from Sewage'. A Royal Commission was set up to investigate the situation. Its first report pointed out that there had been a vague promise by the Prime Minister, Lord Derby, at the time of the 1858 Act that the sewage would be treated before being discharged into the Thames.

The Commission's second report concluded that 'it is neither necessary nor justifiable to discharge the sewage of the Metropolis in its crude state into any part of the Thames'.

Once again *The Times* put its weight behind the campaign, writing in 1885:

> Anybody who has frequented the Thames would, though he has been years away and returned blind, recognise its stream by the dull brooding atmosphere of odours the Metropolitan Board of Works brews from its London sewage.

(Quoted in Halliday, 1999)

The Board of Works was forced to seek a solution. What had been greeted with enthusiasm in the 1860s was no longer acceptable in the 1880s. Settling channels were constructed at Beckton and Crossness to separate off the sludge from the liquid component, which would continue to be discharged into the Thames. Further liquid was extracted mechanically, producing 850 tons of pressed sludge per day. They tried offering it for sale as fertiliser, but it was regarded by local farmers as having little value (in practice, most of the valuable nitrogen content disappears with the liquid part of the sewage). They tried burning it, but this just produced offensive smells. So in 1887 they commissioned a fleet of six sludge vessels. These sailed down the Thames and dumped it out at sea.

Today, even dumping of sewage sludge at sea is regarded as unacceptable and it was prohibited by an EU Directive in 1998. London's sewage sludge continues to be settled out at the Crossness and Beckton sewage treatment works (see Figure 1.19).

Figure 1.19 A modern photograph of Crossness sewage treatment works

However, the science of sludge incineration has improved since the 1880s and it is now burned (odourlessly) in incinerators (see Figure 1.20). The ash is sent to landfill sites.

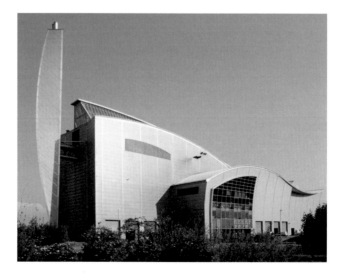

Figure 1.20 Sewage sludge incinerator at Crossness, 2007

3.12   Today's concerns

Today, there is still interest in making agricultural use of sewage sludge, which is rich in potassium and phosphorus. The South American sources of guano have been virtually exhausted and there is concern about global supplies of phosphate rock. Much of Bristol's sewage sludge is sold for fertiliser. Further afield, Sweden has set a national target of recovering 75% of the phosphorus from waste water and other waste streams within the next ten years.

Then there is the question of energy use. When Bazalgette installed steam pumps to raise the sewage, he committed London to keep running them for as long as the system operated. This might be for as long as the city continues to exist. Today the pumps are electrically operated and the concern has shifted to reducing the carbon dioxide emissions associated with this.

It must not be thought that the threat of cholera has disappeared completely. Globally, it is still widespread. An outbreak in 2008 in Zimbabwe had killed over 4000 people by June 2009. It has been particularly bad because the economic collapse in the country had prevented sewage plants from operating properly and deprived hospitals of the necessary medicines for treatment.

Activity 1.7   Bazalgette's scheme in retrospect

Looking back on Bazalgette's scheme from today: Exactly what problems did it solve? What new problems did it create? Who benefited and who lost out?

Discussion

Chadwick's policy of 'the complete purification of the dwelling house, next of the street and lastly of the river' was achieved. The Thames through central London was cleaner and the Houses of Parliament became usable. London's homes could use WCs and the threat of cholera was removed.

The disbenefits were that the sewage was simply dumped further downstream and this did nothing to improve the water quality in the Thames estuary. Travellers up the Thames had to face the 'dull brooding atmosphere of odours that the Metropolitan Board of Works brews from its sewage'. The unfortunate passengers of the *Princess Alice* met a particularly nasty fate. Salmon fishing remained an impossible activity. In 1858 the government chose the cheaper of the two plans on the table, but the 'purification' of 'the Thames Estuary' would have to be carried out 30 years later. Even the dumping of sewage sludge in the sea was eventually considered unacceptable and banned 140 years later in 1998.

The sewers were skilfully designed to run by gravity, but at key points the sewage had to be pumped to a higher level, particularly to enable it to be discharged on the outgoing tide. This created a need for fuel (initially coal) which would last for as long as the system continued to operate.

The scheme stopped the recycling of agricultural nutrients like phosphorus back to the fields. This was fine as long as there were alternative sources, such as imported South American guano. Now these are gone this is a problem that has still largely to be addressed.

Summary of Section 3

This section has described the sewage crisis that developed in London in the 1840s and 1850s, in part due to the adoption of the water closet. It has described the threat of a cholera epidemic and the lack of knowledge at the time about the causes of the disease. It has reflected on the administrative problems that dealing with the problem created and described the data-gathering process and the formulation of suitable technological solutions. It has looked at the role of the press in influencing the political decisions that had to be made during the 'Great Stink' crisis of the summer of 1858. The construction of Bazalgette's intercepting sewer scheme has been described and the question of whether or not it was truly a long-term solution has been considered.

Whatever happened to the London Smog?

4

No Sherlock Holmes adventure is complete without yellow 'pea-soup' fog swirling around soot-blackened buildings. Where is it now? Unlike sewage, where we can point to a major effort to rid the city of a problem, London's air pollution seems to have been something that was tolerated for a very long time and even celebrated in art. Many factors have contributed to its disappearance but it took a serious smog in 1952 to get proper action.

4.1 Coal comes to London

Much of the problem relates to London's fuel supply problems, which seem to have started in the thirteenth century. Despite London being surrounded by heavily wooded landscape, firewood became so expensive that it was necessary to import coal by sea from mines hundreds of miles away in County Durham and around Newcastle.

Although wood when burned produces smoke, Durham 'sea coal' produces a particularly unpleasant acrid form. It contains about 1% sulphur and, when burned, this is converted into the acidic gas sulphur dioxide (SO_2). Wood, on the other hand, is almost sulphur free. The pollution from coal was considered sufficiently bad for a proclamation to be issued in 1306 banning its use in London, but this was simply ignored. As the city grew, so did its coal consumption: 24 000 tons in 1585 and 216 000 tons in 1650. By 1680 there were 1400 ships simply carrying coal from Newcastle to London.

In the mid-seventeenth century the environmental campaigner John Evelyn (see Box 1.5) wrote that London was cloaked in:

> Such a cloud of sea-coal, as if there be a resemblence of hell upon earth, it is in this volcano in a foggy day: this pestilent smoak, which corrodes the very yron [iron], and spoils all the moveables, leaving a soot on all things that it lights: and so fatally seizing on the lungs of the inhabitants, that cough and consumption spare no man.

> *(Quoted in Brimblecombe, 1987)*

Evelyn petitioned King Charles II unsuccessfully for what today would be called 'zoning': to have industry moved out of the city and further down the Thames. However, his ideas on the construction of parks with sweet-smelling flowers did have an impact and, to this day, central London has a large number of them.

London's air certainly could be fatal. Like other places surrounded by marshland, London had 'ordinary' fogs. But just occasionally it also had 'great stinking fogs', as recorded in John Gadbury's diary of London

Box 1.5   John Evelyn

Figure 1.21 John Evelyn (1620–1706)

Evelyn was a prolific reader and writer whose motto was 'explore everything, keep the best'. His best known work, *Sylva, or, a Discourse on Forest-trees*, was written to encourage landowners to plant timber for the expanding navy. He was an early campaigner for 'town planning' and the need for urban parks. His 1661 treatise *Fumifugium* petitioned King Charles II about the problems of London's air pollution. He also wrote a plan for the reconstruction of London after the Great Fire of 1666.

weather between 1668 and 1689. Today we would call these '**smogs**', a combination of smoke and fog. Two of these happened in November 1679. Records of death rates showed an increase in mortality, particularly from what was described as 'tisick', a breathing disorder.

The problem was the sheer number of coal fires. Almost every home burned coal, as did every factory. As London's role as an industrial centre increased, so did its coal consumption; to almost 700 000 tons in 1750.

The mixture of black soot and sulphur dioxide took its toll on London buildings. The surface layers of limestone, and particularly the fine carved ornamentation, were eaten away by acid rainwater. The white lead oxide pigment used in paints of the time was blackened by the sulphur. Some eighteenth-century leases for houses in fashionable districts required that their exteriors were repainted three times a year.

4.2   Experiments in efficiency and smokeless fuels

Was it necessary to burn so much coal? Could it be done more efficiently and without making so much smoke? In the late eighteenth century the American Count Rumford carefully specified household fireplace designs for maximum heating efficiency, with a 'throat' above the grate and a fireclay surround angled to reflect the heat into the room. Another American, Benjamin Franklin, emphasised that unburnt smoke was wasted fuel.

When the Royal Navy adopted steam power for its ships in the 1840s, they had no wish for their position to be given away by plumes of smoke. They recommended 'smokeless' anthracite. This is a high-quality, clean-burning form of coal, almost pure carbon with very little sulphur, and was accordingly more expensive.

The development of railways in the 1830s and 1840s not only increased the demand for coal but provided an alternative route for supplying it to London from the mines in the north of England and in Wales. Steam engines could also power new large ships to bring ever more coal to London; almost six million tons by 1865 and nine million by 1877. Although London, in theory, had a choice of a range of fuels (see Box 1.6), ordinary 'sea coal' was cheap, and for most applications the fuel of choice.

Box 1.6   Victorian London's fuels

Wood

This was treated as a desirable, low-sulphur, fuel but it was in short supply in London from about 1300 onwards. Although it produces smoke when burned, this was regarded as less offensive than that produced by coal.

Charcoal

This is produced by heating wood to a high temperature to drive off all the volatile gases, leaving a low-sulphur, smokeless fuel that is almost pure carbon. In Victorian times it would have been done by 'charcoal burners' in the forests. It was in high demand for smelting iron and glass making, so would have been expensive.

Sea coal (also known as bituminous coal or 'house coal')

Coal brought by sea to London from the thirteenth century onwards from mines near Newcastle and later from Wales. This was cheaper than wood or charcoal but contains sulphur. It contains a certain amount of tarry or 'bituminous' matter which makes it easy to ignite and helps it burn with a bright flame. It is not 'smokeless'.

Anthracite

A hard coal, mostly from mines in Wales. This is almost pure carbon, like charcoal, and is low in sulphur. As a smokeless fuel it was in high demand for the Royal Navy, railways and industry, and more expensive than ordinary coal. It is hard to ignite so was unpopular for domestic use.

Town gas

A mixture of carbon monoxide and hydrogen made at gasworks dotted through the city by heating coal. Commercially introduced in London in 1812, it was initially just a lighting fuel. It was reasonably smokeless in the home, but much pollution took place at the local gasworks where much of the sulphur was extracted. The piles of sulphur contributed to the distinctive 'gasworks' odour. As a fuel, town gas was several times the price of coal but very convenient to use.

Coke

The remaining solid fuel after the town gas had been produced. This is a smokeless fuel but has a high percentage of ash, making it difficult to ignite and burn, reducing its popularity in homes. It was mainly used in industry.

Electricity

Mains electricity was introduced in London in the 1880s. Initially it was very expensive and only used for lighting. During the 1890s and the early twentieth century it started to power trams and railways and electric motors in factories, replacing small steam engines.

SAQ 1.4   Smokeless and low-sulphur fuels

Below is a list of domestic heating fuels available in Victorian times. Are they smokeless and/or low-sulphur fuels?

Wood, charcoal, sea coal, anthracite, coke.

4.3   Opaque legislation

While it was obvious that smoke was not good for the health, it was not clear how to legislate against it. Coal smoke was 'bad' but wood smoke was somehow 'better'. It was also difficult for individual householders to complain about smoke from local industry when their own household fires and lighting produced smoke as well. Smoke was regarded as a 'public nuisance' rather than a public health risk and legislation concentrated on industrial emissions of 'black' smoke, implying that smoke of other shades was relatively harmless. There was little attention paid to the sulphur content of coal and no legislation about domestic fires.

This was all in marked contrast to the 1863 Alkali Act legislation covering the emissions of acid hydrogen chloride gas from chemical factories producing washing soda. This gas had a visible, devastating effect on the local vegetation. The Act forced factories to fit *flue gas scrubbers*, giving cleaner air, but at the price of washing the acid into the local rivers instead.

The lack of clear legislation suited the industrial 'smoke makers' even though they were lampooned in the press (Figure 1.22).

IMPORTANT MEETING OF SMOKE MAKERS.

Figure 1.22 The industrial smoke-making culprits are lampooned in *Punch* in 1853

There were cases where local pressure worked. For example, Meux's brewery in Tottenham Court Road was forced to use smokeless fuel after complaints from local residents about the black smoke that it produced. However, successful court cases were rare and fines were minimal.

4.4   Black light

Coal fires were not the only source of air pollution. Soot (see Box 1.7) was an essential ingredient of Victorian lighting, which was based on the naked flames of candles and oil and gas lamps. In these the light is actually emitted from a continuous stream of glowing, fine, unburned particles of carbon within the flame (see Figure 1.23). Town gas was originally carefully formulated to burn with a bright flame and was not sold on its heat content as gas is today.

This is a very inefficient way of turning fuel into light, in part because so much of the fuel is left unburned and ends up being emitted as greasy soot. Modern electric lighting with fluorescent lamps is about 100 times more fuel efficient! In real terms (i.e. compared with the cost of food), artificial

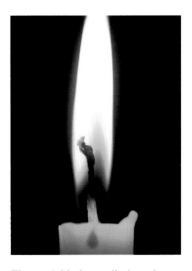

Figure 1.23 A candle burning; the light comes from fine, glowing, unburned particles of carbon

lighting was over a hundred times more expensive in the nineteenth century than it is today (Fouquet, 2008). As a result, after sunset most homes were very poorly lit and coal fires provided a valuable source of light as well as heat.

4.5   Education: the Fog and Smoke Committee

The winter of 1879/1880 was particularly bad. December 1879 was the foggiest month on record by that time. The Registrar General, responsible for statistics of births and deaths, commented on the high death rate during fogs and estimated that they had caused the premature death of about 3000 people. His opinions had very little effect on Parliament.

Given the lack of interest in legislation, Ernest Hart, editor of the *British Medical Journal*, and Octavia Hill, an advocate of open spaces for fresh air (and co-founder of the National Trust), set up the Fog and Smoke Committee. This tried to tackle the problem through a campaign of education and awareness. In November 1881 they held a Smoke Abatement Exhibition in Kensington with 230 exhibits. Most of the interest was on the domestic side.

This was certainly an uphill struggle. At the time the coal fire was widely used for both heating and cooking and was the focal centre of the home (see Figure 1.24). Given the expense of other forms of illumination, the flames were also an essential source of light. If the fire used Durham coal, which tends to 'cake' as it burns, it required regular attention with a metal poker to keep it burning brightly.

Figure 1.24 A re-creation of a Victorian/early twentieth-century working-class living room at the Beamish Museum in County Durham. The 'open, pokeable coal fire was used for both heating and cooking and was also a useful source of light. The gas cooker to the left started competing in the 1890s.

At the Smoke Abatement Exhibition, stoves for burning smokeless fuel were demonstrated and critically reviewed. These could be significantly more efficient than open fires (modern figures suggest a factor of two). Figure 1.25 shows some examples.

Figure 1.25 Heating stoves available in the late nineteenth century *(Source: CIBSE, 1998)*

There were problems with acceptability. Smokeless fuel was usually difficult to ignite. A large quantity would be loaded into the stove, lit (sometimes with a special gas burner), and when it was well ablaze the fire would be regulated by closing the doors and restricting the air supply. Even with mica windows in the doors, this meant that the flames could not be clearly seen, nor could the rosy glow of the fire light a room. The public remained firmly in favour of an 'open, pokeable, companionable fire' even if it did use more coal.

In 1884 a bill was put before Parliament to regulate the emission of smoke from all new buildings in London. It was voted down.

Box 1.7   Victorian air pollutants

Soot

Visible smoke consists mainly of particles of unburned carbon or soot, but contaminated with other chemicals. Large particles of soot may be obvious as 'smuts' on clean clothing and can be measured as an annual 'sootfall' in grams falling on a square metre of an outdoor collecting plate (g per m^2).

Smoke and particulates

Smoke may also contain very fine 'particulates', such as the unburned soot from a candle flame (or from a car engine). Modern statistics concentrate on **PM10s**, *particulates* smaller than 10 micrometres in diameter (one micrometre is 1/1000th of a millimetre), which can be breathed in. Statistics quote average densities in terms of micrograms per cubic metre of air (μg per m^3).

Sulphur dioxide

Fuels such as coal (and oil) often contain significant quantities of sulphur (up to 5%). When burned this produces the acidic gas sulphur dioxide (SO_2). In the human body this attacks the lining of the lungs. It also attacks fabrics, the white lead oxide pigment in Victorian paint, and building materials, particularly limestone. Modern measurements give statistics in terms of average densities quoted in micrograms per cubic metre of air (μg per m^3).

London fogs were largely regarded as a necessary unavoidable consequence of industrial society. Many, such as the French painter Monet and the American poet James Russell Lowell, actually thought them quite artistic (see Box 1.8).

Box 1.8   Is it art?

The French impressionist painter Monet deliberately chose to visit London in winter to carry out his paintings of the Thames (see Figure 1.26). 'Without fog,' he said, 'London would not be a beautiful city. It is the fog that gives it its magnificent breadth.'

Figure 1.26 Claude Monet, *The Houses of Parliament, Sunset*, 1903

The American poet James Russell Lowell enthused about a London fog in 1883:

We are in the beginning of our foggy season, and today are having a yellow fog, and that always enlivens me […] It is very picturesque also. Even the cabs are rimmed with a halo, and people across the way have all that possibility of suggestion which piques the fancy so in the figures of fading frescoes. Even the gray, even the black fogs make a new and unexplored world not unpleasing to one who is getting palled with familiar landscapes.

(Quoted in Brimblecombe, 1987)

Despite the lack of new legislation, the message of the smoke abatement campaigners may have had an effect because the number of days with fogs appears to have reached its peak in the 1890s (see Figure 1.27).

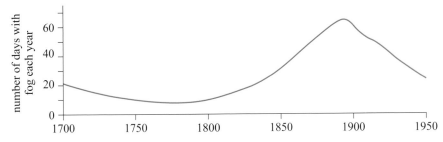

Figure 1.27 Number of days with fogs 1700–1950 *(Source: redrawn from Brimblecombe, 1987)*

There are perhaps many reasons for this, but in part it may be due to the increased use of the 'manufactured fuels' town gas and electricity substituting for the direct use of coal.

4.6   New technologies arrive

By the 1890s rising real wages and promotion of 'penny in the slot' meters meant that more people could afford gas for cooking and lighting, replacing some of the need for coal fires. Also small gasworks were being replaced with larger, cleaner and more efficient ones.

Mains electricity was also introduced in London in the late 1880s. Initially it was extremely expensive, but the newly invented incandescent light bulbs had the potential to compete with gas lighting. When the gas industry fought back with its own new technology (see below) the electricity industry diversified into motive power. Electric trains started to replace inefficient smoky steam power and factories started to replace individual steam engines with electric motors. The electricity itself was generated in large power stations powered by coal. It might be thought that this would produce even more smoke, but the electricity industry was locked in cut-throat competition with the gas industry for the lighting market. Using coal with maximum efficiency (and minimum wasted fuel) was critical for both of them.

This is not to say that they were spotless. When, in 1905, the new Underground Electric Railways of London Ltd built a (smoky) new power station, Chelsea Borough Council's court action against them failed because the generating station was able to claim that their smoke was not so much 'black' as 'dark brown'!

Gas lighting and even town gas itself changed. Instead of using a naked flame to produce light, gas was now used to heat a 'gas mantle' a thin gauze coated with 'rare earth' chemicals that glowed when hot (these are still used in modern gas camping lamps). The process for producing town gas was changed to ensure complete combustion and maximum heat output. The efficiency of gas lighting rose by a factor of four, making it cheaper and giving it a whole new economic lease of life, much to the dismay of the competing electricity companies.

SAQ 1.5   Smoke legislation

Why was nineteenth-century smoke legislation so ineffective?

4.7   Air quality measurements and years of slow improvements

One fundamental problem for the pursuit of 'clean air' was the lack of actual measurements of exactly how dirty it was. The arrival of the twentieth century brought more interest in air quality measurement championed by the medical journal *The Lancet*. Early measurements in 1912 with 'sootfall' gauges suggested that 76 000 tons of soot fell on the administrative county of London every year (about a quarter of a kilogram for every square metre!). By 1918 an automatic device had been perfected that could measure the suspended smoke concentration in the air. Automatic monitoring of sulphur dioxide levels followed in 1928, with further improvements in equipment over the following years.

Measurements of sootfall and smoke showed a slow improvement in London's air quality throughout the 1920s and 30s even though industry continued to emit various shades of smoke into the atmosphere (see, for example, Figure 1.28).

Figure 1.28 The chimneys of the Tate & Lyle Sugar Refinery, Silvertown, 1939

On the domestic front, gas cooking took over from coal. It was estimated that by 1942 over 80% of Londoners were cooking with gas. The increased gas use also meant a greater availability of coke for smokeless stoves. In 1936 it was being sold for 20% less than the price of coal and domestic coke fires were being installed in southern England at the rate of 100 000 a year (Davidson, 1982). Electricity was also falling in price, becoming more affordable and replacing gas lighting in the home.

SAQ 1.6   Lighting technologies and soot production

How did new lighting technologies reduce the production of soot?

Even so, London remained prepared for thick fogs where visibility might drop to a matter of feet. It was only in the 1930s that London buses were permitted by the Metropolitan Police to have windscreens, and even then they had to be openable to improve vision in fog.

4.8   The smog of December 1952

A real turning point in the campaign for clean air came in December 1952. A serious smog occurred which hung over the city for four very cold and almost windless days. Visibility dropped dramatically (see Figure 1.29). Smoke and sulphur dioxide levels, as recorded by automatic equipment in 12 different locations, rose rapidly. Figure 1.30 shows the average figures, but the smog varied in density across the city and was worse in some locations than others. The smoke density at County Hall, opposite the Houses of Parliament, reached almost 4500 µg per m^3 on the 7th and 8th of December. Only on the 9th of December did the wind pick up and the pollution levels fall.

The first reported casualties of the smog were cattle at the Smithfield Agricultural Show. An Aberdeen Angus died, 12 other cattle had to be slaughtered, and 160 needed veterinary treatment. All were relatively

Figure 1.29 A London bus struggles through the 1952 smog guided by a man with a flare

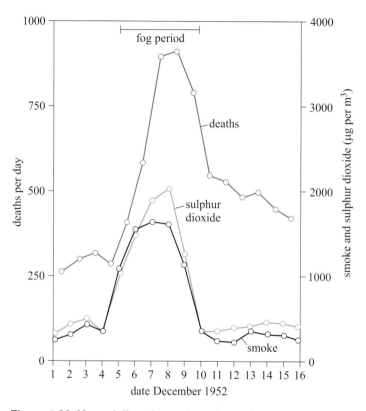

Figure 1.30 Mean daily values of smoke and sulphur dioxide during the London smog of 1952, and numbers of deaths *(Source: redrawn from Brimblecombe, 1987)*

young and in prime condition. At Sadler's Wells, an opera had to be abandoned after the first act because the theatre was so full of smog.

Human health problems soon followed, with a soaring death rate. This was mainly due to heart and lung disease, with over 90% of the deaths being in people over the age of 45. Also the number of deaths in children under one year of age doubled. The illnesses were unusually sudden in onset, typically on the third or fourth day of the smog. Patients suffered from shortness of breath, some fever and an excess of fluid in the lungs. The death rate remained high for several weeks after the air quality improved.

The Ministry of Health concluded that it had caused approximately 4000 excess deaths, due to respiratory and cardiovascular disease. This estimate was higher than for any previous smog. The true figure may have been even higher because the analysis used a rather short cut-off time. Later investigations showed that it was the combination of smoke and SO_2 that made the effects particularly lethal. This is sometimes called the 'cocktail' effect.

SAQ 1.7   Analysis of deaths during the London smog of 1952

Table 1.1 shows detailed data on deaths for the London County Council area. Complete it to show the number of excess deaths in the week after the smog. Suggest why the total number of deaths might have been higher.

Table 1.1 Mortality in the London smog of 1952 (County of London)

Cause	Seasonal norm (deaths per week)	Deaths in week after smog	Excess deaths
Bronchitis	75	704	
Other lung diseases	98	366	
Coronary heart disease, myocardial degeneration	206	525	
Other diseases	508	889	
Total	887	2484	

4.9   The 1956 Clean Air Act

The severity of the smog and the alarming statistics firmly made the link between air pollution and ill health in the minds of the public. The London County Council wrote a damning report. The government was initially dismissive. Iain Macleod, the Minister for Health, was reported in the *Evening Standard* as protesting: 'Really you know, anyone would think fog had only started in London since I became a Minister.' However, it was pressed into setting up an inquiry, the Beaver Committee. Its 1954 report concluded that:

> The domestic fire is the biggest single smoke producer. In ratio to the coal burnt, it produces twice as much smoke as industry and discharges it at a lower level.

(Quoted in GLA, 2002)

This was the first time that the finger of blame had clearly been pointed at domestic pollution. Fortunately, the technology to cure the problem was to hand, as it had been ever since the 1880s. Domestic coal fires could be converted to use readily available smokeless fuel. Real wages had risen enormously since the end of the nineteenth century and heating whole homes with town gas (by now smokeless and largely sulphur free) was an affordable option. Cheaper gas cooking and electric lighting had robbed the open fireplace of its central focus in the home and the new technology of television was displacing it even further.

Any government lethargy in enacting the committee's recommendations was cut short by a Private Member's Bill introduced in Parliament by the Conservative MP Gerald Nabarro. The whole topic became an issue in the General Election of 1955, with both the Conservative and Labour parties promising to take action. The incoming Conservative government introduced their own bill, which became the Clean Air Act of 1956.

For the first time, legislation attempted to control domestic sources of pollution in London as well as those of industry. It did not attempt to tackle it on a city-wide scale but at the level of local authorities, the borough

(a)

(b)

Figure 1.31 (a) Grants became available for domestic stoves like this to burn smokeless fuel. Note the mica windows so that the flames can still be seen and the adjustment knob to regulate the air flow to the fire. **(b)** Smokeless solid fuels such as 'Coalite', a form of coke, were promoted

councils who were the (somewhat larger) successors to the vestries of the mid-nineteenth century. It gave powers to them to set up 'smokeless zones' in which only smokeless fuels would be permitted. Grants were made available to allow people to buy domestic stoves specifically designed to burn smokeless fuel (see Figure 1.31). Even this legislation had already been pioneered in Manchester and Coventry in the late 1940s. There could be no excuses.

Although the Clean Air Act did not actually force local authorities to act, most of them chose to do so. By 1969, when the newly created Greater London Council reviewed the effectiveness of smoke control, it found that over 60 per cent of premises and over 50 per cent of its administrative area had been covered.

As for industrial pollution, the Act was restricted to smoke but it prohibited 'dark smoke' (and clearly defined what that meant). Large urban industrial users could use smokeless fuel or fit scrubbers to their chimneys to remove the soot. The newly constructed 'B' section of Battersea Power Station, which ran on coal, was equipped with flue gas scrubbers (see Figure 1.32). These washed both the soot and sulphur dioxide out with Thames river water. As with the alkali legislation of 1863, this had the effect of cleaning the air, but at the expense of a dirtier Thames!

Figure 1.32 Battersea Power Station in 1971. Much of the 'smoke' is actually water vapour produced after the soot and SO_2 in the flue gases had been washed out into the Thames

Box 1.9 summarises changes in the air quality in London over time.

Box 1.9	Timeline: Cleaning up London's air
1300s	Coal imports to London start from Newcastle
1660s	John Evelyn campaigns to move industry out of the city
1790s	Count Rumford improves fireplace design
1800	London uses over 1 million tons of coal a year
1812	Town gas introduced in London
1840s	Royal Navy experiments with 'smokeless' anthracite
1865	London uses 6 million tons of coal a year
1881	Smoke Abatement Exhibition
1880s	Mains electricity introduced in London
1887	London uses 12 million tons of coal a year
1890s	Possible peak of London fogs
1912	Measurements of 'sootfall' begin
1952	Serious smog kills over 4000 in weeks
1956	Clean Air Act introduces 'Smokeless Zones'
1970	Use of house coal in London almost ceases
1970s	Natural gas from the North Sea replaces town gas

4.10   Re-imagining London as clean

There is perhaps a deeper reason why the Clean Air Act finally came to fruition in 1956. It was a time of 're-imagining' both London and its homes. There was no longer an army of domestic servants to endlessly light coal fires and clean up ash. Nor was this considered a proper part of 1950s housework. The Second World War had destroyed a large part of London, particularly the industrial areas and slums of the East End and Dockland. The post-war period was one of building a 'new brighter future'. Much of this was expressed in the 1951 Festival of Britain, held on the South Bank almost opposite the Houses of Parliament. This exhibition of arts and industry was intended to echo the Great Exhibition of 1851 and the Festival Hall, built at the time, remains to this day (see Figure 1.33). This 'new age' spirit continued with the Coronation of Queen Elizabeth II in 1953.

Pre-war attitudes had baulked at legislation over what individuals did in their own homes and how they lived their lives. However, the war had forced legislation on such things as food rationing, which was seen as socially acceptable. The 1950s were a time when 'doing away with that form of liberty […] the sacred power to poison to death not only themselves but their neighbours', as Dr Snow had put it in 1849, may have become more acceptable.

(a)   (b)

Figure 1.33 (a) Artwork from the 1951 Festival of Britain; (b) the newly built Royal Festival Hall

4.11   London's air after the Clean Air Act

The effects of the Clean Air Act can be seen in London's fuel use (Figure 1.34). Prior to 1956 coal supplied about 60% of London's energy, and half of that was house coal. By 1970 the use of house coal in London had almost completely died out.

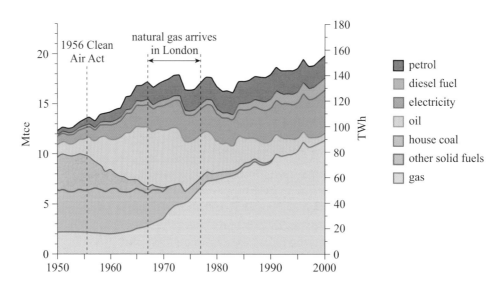

Figure 1.34 London energy use 1950–2000, 1 TWh = 1000 million kWh, 1 Mtce = 1 million tons of coal equivalent *(Source: adapted from GLA, 2002)*

What is perhaps remarkable is that the use of other solid fuels did not increase. Instead there was an increased use of gas and electricity for heating and a switch to heating oil, both of which had become more affordable during the 1950s and 60s. Although heating oil was a 'smokeless' fuel it did still contain sulphur and its removal had to wait for European legislation in 1999.

In the 1960s large discoveries of natural gas were made in the North Sea. In 1967 the decision was made to convert the whole UK gas system to this from town gas. The process took ten years. Natural gas is a smokeless, low-sulphur fuel. It is almost pure methane and because it has different combustion properties from town gas, its adoption meant that almost every gas appliance had to be fitted with new burners. This was a task that required an army of gas fitters so that conversion could be carried out with minimal interruption.

North Sea gas was priced to be cheaper than town gas. This, together with the high oil prices between 1973 and 1986, saw a surge in the installation of gas-fired central heating. By 2000 this had almost wiped out the use of solid fuel and heating oil in homes and offices in London.

A chart of London's average smoke and sulphur dioxide concentrations (Figure 1.35) is revealing. By 1970 average smoke concentrations were down by a factor of five and sulphur dioxide levels by almost a factor of three from those of 1956. Even those had been a considerable improvement on likely levels in the 1890s.

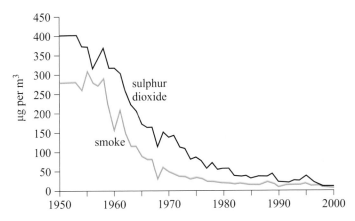

Figure 1.35 Average smoke and sulphur dioxide levels in London 1950–2000. Note that before 1954 data was only published as 5-year averages. *(Source: redrawn from GLA, 2002)*

The last major 'pea-soup' smog in London was in 1962.

Activity 1.8   Why wasn't there a Clean Air Act in the 1880s?

In 1858 Parliament had rushed through an Act of Parliament to deal with London's sewage. In the 1880s the Fog and Smoke Committee were campaigning for action on London air pollution. Yet in 1884 Parliament actually voted down a bill to curb smoke emissions from new buildings.

Why did London have to wait for another 70 years for a Clean Air Act? How had homes and attitudes changed by 1956?

Discussion

There are many possible factors:

Continuous measurements of air pollution did not start until the early twentieth century. The effects of the 1952 smog in pollution terms were carefully monitored. The link between pollution and the death rate could be clearly seen.

The number of excess deaths in 1952 was higher than in any previous smog.

The Beaver Report clearly stated that the problem was with domestic fires. This had never been said before.

In the 1880s there were still many like J. Toulmin Smith in the 1850s who championed the freedom of the individual against the interference of government. By the 1950s two world wars had necessitated much 'interfering' legislation about what people could or could not do in their homes. Legislation about what fuels they might burn was not so much of an intrusion on individual liberty.

Smokeless stoves had been available since the 1880s, but did not have public acceptability. They did not fit in with the image of the fireplace as the visible centre of the home. By the 1950s most London households had switched to gas for cooking. Electric lighting was much more affordable. The role of the visible 'open fire' as the centre of the home had been eroded (and was being replaced by the television!). Also the increased use of gas made smokeless fuel more available than it was in the 1880s.

Summary of Section 4

In this section we have looked at the long-term problem of London's air pollution, particularly that from coal smoke and soot. We have looked at the relative ineffectiveness of nineteenth-century legislation, particularly about smoke from domestic fires. We have considered the available heating fuels in Victorian London and their relative performance as 'smokeless' and 'low-sulphur' fuels. We have looked at the role of the open fire as the focus of the Victorian home and the problems of the acceptability of smokeless stoves in the 1880s. We have considered the development of air quality measurement in the early twentieth century and the influence of new technologies such as electric lighting and the gas mantle in reducing smoke. We have looked at how the crisis of the smog of December 1952 finally produced effective legislation, the Clean Air Act of 1956. Finally, we have looked at the effects of this Act and the introduction of North Sea gas in the 1970s in dramatically improving London's air quality.

Lessons from London's past

5

The Great Stink and the London smogs illustrate that there is a sequence of necessary steps in dealing with a pollution problem as set out in Figure 1.36.

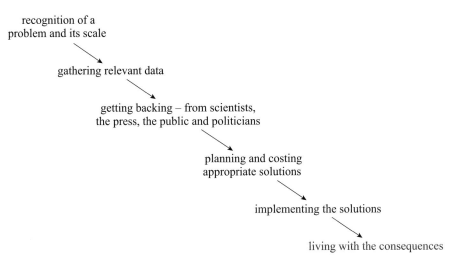

Figure 1.36 Possible steps in solving an environmental problem

5.1   Recognition of a problem and its scale

London's sewage became a problem in the early nineteenth century when the increased use of the water closet upset the existing mechanism for recycling night-soil back to the fields and washed it into the Thames instead. It was recognised as a city-wide rather than a local problem and in 1848 the Metropolitan Commission of Sewers was set up to investigate.

The problem of London's air pollution had been recognised and stated many times over from the thirteenth century onwards. In the 1660s John Evelyn saw it as city-wide and petitioned King Charles II to have 'zoning' introduced in London.

5.2   Gathering relevant data

For data on London's sewage we can thank Edwin Chadwick, who was a master of gathering information on social conditions, particularly of the poor, and writing hard-hitting reports to Parliament. Researchers like Dr John Snow carefully documented just how dangerous a disease cholera was (and still is today).

Hard data on London's air pollution had to wait until the early twentieth century for the appropriate measurement equipment to be developed. Where did the pollution come from? The 1954 Beaver Committee clearly said that the problem was domestic coal fires and that meant that it was coming from a large percentage of London homes.

5.3   Getting backing from scientists, the public, the press and politicians

The case for action on London's sewage had support from the highest scientific level, particularly Michael Faraday, Professor of Chemistry at the Royal Institution. The rapid action on the 'Great Stink' was spurred on by *The Times* newspaper and the magazine *Punch*.

Action on air pollution was championed for many years by the *British Medical Journal* and *The Lancet*. It eventually became an issue in the 1955 General Election.

5.4   Planning and costing appropriate solutions

There was no shortage of proposals to deal with London's sewage. Indeed, Joseph Bazalgette was originally employed to sort through 137 of them! His job was to work out the fine detail of just one. Who would do the work? His city-wide technological solution required a new body, the Metropolitan Board of Works, to be set up. How much would it cost? His estimate was £2.5 million.

The solutions for London's air pollution were explored at the 1881 Smoke Abatement Exhibition. By 1936 smokeless stoves had become sufficiently popular to be installed at the rate of 100 000 a year in southern England. Smokeless zones were tried out in Manchester and Coventry in the late 1940s.

5.5   Implementing the solutions

This is perhaps the most difficult part. In both cases it has required a crisis to get decisive action.

In 1855 Parliament had passed a bill that said that *none* of London's sewage should go into the Thames. The 1858 Great Stink forced Parliament to backtrack and say that Bazalgette's £2.5 million scheme was good enough. Who would pay for it? The money would be borrowed (but with a Treasury guarantee) and paid back by London ratepayers over 40 years.

Although anti-smoke legislation had been passed in the nineteenth century it had only a limited effect. The 1952 smog embarrassed the government sufficiently for it to create the 1956 Clean Air Act. Who would administer its enforcement? Local authorities (i.e. borough councils). Who would pay for smokeless stoves? The householder, but with the help of council grants. Would it be expensive? Probably not. There was plenty of cheap coke, and alternatives like gas heating were much more affordable than they had been in the past.

5.6   Living with the consequences

Bazalgette's sewage scheme of 1858 was not entirely satisfactory. Dumping untreated sewage in the Thames had to be stopped in the 1880s and dumping sewage sludge in the sea was banned in 1998. The sewage pumps continue to consume energy to this day.

As for air pollution, the new fuel of natural gas has swept away much of the issue of smoke and sulphur dioxide. However, UK North Sea gas production peaked in the year 2000 and the UK can look forward to being dependent on imports for 75% of its energy needs by 2020.

Often, when a new environmental crisis appears, there is a cry of 'Why doesn't the government *do* something?' Hopefully these examples show that action has to be preceded by much research and extraordinary amounts of argument. Nothing seems to be simple. On the brighter side, it must be said that both Bazalgette's sewage scheme and the 1956 Clean Air Act produced dramatic environmental improvements within 20 years of their respective crises.

Summary of Section 5

This section has set out a number of steps in the 'solution' of an environmental problem and considered how these relate to the events of our two examples from London's past.

6 London after the stink and the smog: a new age with new problems

6.1 Urban sprawl

Time marches on and London has continued to expand. Improved transport in the twentieth century, electric trams and trolleybuses, motor buses and the electrification of the railways have all made commuting easier. London has continued to swell in size. In 1965 a new administrative area was created, Greater London, covering over 600 square miles, five times the area of the 1889 Inner London designation. In 2007 the population of the Greater London area was over 7.5 million.

This is not the whole picture. In many ways most towns within 50 miles of London are, in part, commuter suburbs and the true population of the wider London conurbation is probably about 12 million people. For many purposes, such as air quality, 'London' is treated as being that area within the M25 motorway, completed in 1986 (see Figure 1.37).

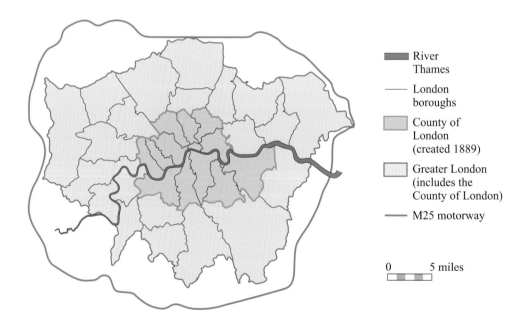

Figure 1.37 A 2004 map showing 'Greater London' and 'London', as defined for air quality purposes, within the M25 motorway

6.2   Acid rain and 'pollution elsewhere'

New technologies have appeared, and with them their pollution consequences. As shown in Figure 1.34, London's electricity consumption has continued to grow, but this has not meant more power stations in the city. The National Grid, originally constructed in the 1930s, has increasingly been used to supply electricity from distant power stations. In particular, electricity made from coal could be imported from enormous stations located close to the coal mines in the north of England or in Wales. Although this has helped in the local drive to clean London's air, it has meant that the pollution, and particularly that from sulphur dioxide, has just been displaced to another part of the country. This is sometimes called 'pollution elsewhere'; a technology may be clean at the point of use, but dirty somewhere else conveniently out of sight and mind.

In fact the SO_2 emissions have been so large that they have been carried right across the North Sea to Scandinavia to fall as 'acid rain'. London's pollution problems have become not just a city-wide one, but an international one. This issue was tackled by pan-European legislation in the 1990s requiring that a proportion of UK coal-fired power stations are fitted with flue gas desulphurisation (FGD) equipment to cut their SO_2 emissions.

6.3   The rise of the private motor car

In the 1950s private car ownership in the UK was very low. Fuel use in private transport has risen fivefold since then. The increases in petrol and diesel fuel use in London are also shown in Figure 1.34. As pollution from coal smoke has disappeared from London, new pollution from car use has risen in importance. Motor vehicles, particularly diesel engines, produce sooty particulates, and both petrol and diesel engines can produce acidic nitrogen oxides. Indeed, the new London smog is now more likely to take the form of a brown acid haze on a hot summer's day than a pea-soup fog in winter. This type of pollution has resulted in 1990s legislation for the fitting of catalytic converters to all new petrol cars and strict engine management controls on diesel ones.

6.4   Carbon dioxide and global warming

Although London has been burning fossil fuels for centuries, and producing carbon dioxide, their global use has increased rapidly since the Second World War. About a half of all human CO_2 emissions from burning fossil fuels have been produced since 1975. This is a pollution issue whose importance was pointed out in the late 1980s. In this case London's pollution and its contribution to climate change has become not just an international problem but a global one. This is the topic for the next part of this block.

Activity 1.9   Your home as a museum exhibit

Look back at Figure 1.24 (in Section 4). It shows a museum reconstruction of a late Victorian/early twentieth century working-class home. Imagine your home as it might be portrayed in a museum 100 years in the future. What do you regard as the 'focus' of your home? What might the exhibit contain to illustrate the clear differences from the Victorian home and possible homes of the future?

Discussion

The 'focus' of mine seems to be a gas fire (not flame effect!) and a small 1990s TV. There are some comfortable armchairs facing them. It's also got assorted CD and DVD players and some 1970s hi-fi equipment. There is a lot of computer equipment and piles of books and paper (Edwin Chadwick would feel at home!). Since this is a museum exhibit I would want to show the 1990s telephone/fax/answering machine and that the room is lit by low-energy compact fluorescent light bulbs. I would also show that cooking is done in a separate kitchen using a gas cooker and that I have a WC and a bathroom with an acrylic bath. I suppose that to distinguish it from homes of 100 years in the future I should point out that the walls have got only 50 mm of insulation and the windows are only 2008 vintage double glazing.

Summary of Part 1

In this part we have reflected on the nature of cities and their reasons for existence. We looked briefly at the reasons for the current location of London and at its growth, particularly during the nineteenth century.

Sections 3 and 4 described how London has had to face up to two pollution problems: that of sewage, culminating in the crisis of the 'Great Stink' of 1858, and the longer-term one of air pollution and smogs resulting in the Clean Air Act of 1956.

In Section 5 we looked at the steps involved in dealing with these two environmental problems which have, to a certain extent, led to 'solutions'.

Finally, Section 6 has briefly described how London has continued to grow and some more recent environmental concerns.

After completing Part 1 you should:

- appreciate the importance of cities for sustainability
- recognise that population density and resource use in cities pose environmental problems
- be aware that environmental problems have been addressed only where there is political/economic/social will
- appreciate that solutions from the past can inform current problems and offer solutions
- recognise the factors that influence change.

Answers to SAQs

SAQ 1.1

London was sited on a large river and became the centre of communication links by road and sea. More specifically, London was at the lowest bridging point on the Thames. Watling Street was the strategic road from Dover (and Rome) to the south, and to the heart of England to the north. The Thames at this point was deep enough to unload seagoing ships and there was convenient high ground on which to build a city.

SAQ 1.2

WCs flushed waste out of the home (and out of mind). Homes no longer required smelly individual cesspools. The increased sales of water pleased the private water companies. Night-soil was no longer recycled to the fields, depriving the 'nightmen' of trade and market gardens of fertiliser. It was now transported via the sewers, which had to be enlarged (at the taxpayers' expense), to the Thames, now a 'great cesspool'. There it killed the fish stocks and created problems for those water companies who took their water from the river.

SAQ 1.3

If they believed in the 'miasmatic theory' and Chadwick's statement that 'all smell is disease', they might be very worried about catching cholera. If they did catch it then they could be dead in a matter of hours.

SAQ 1.4

Fuel*	Smokeless?	Low sulphur?
Wood	No	Yes
Charcoal	Yes	Yes
Durham sea coal	No	No
Anthracite	Yes	Yes
Coke	Yes	Yes

Town gas has been omitted since it started out as a relatively smoky and sulphur-laden fuel in early Victorian times, but by the early 20th century it had become a much cleaner product.

SAQ 1.5

It did not apply to domestic fires.

It treated smoke pollution as a matter of 'public nuisance' rather than 'public health'.

It legislated against 'black smoke' without clearly defining what that meant.

SAQ 1.6

Candles, oil lamps and naked gas flames all relied on fine, glowing particles of unburnt carbon to produce light. Electric light did not produce soot (except at the power station!). Gas lighting changed to use a glowing gas mantle and the gas itself had been reformulated for complete combustion.

SAQ 1.7

The excess deaths are: bronchitis, 629; other lung diseases, 268; coronary heart disease, 319; other diseases, 381.

The total number of excess deaths suggested by the data amounts to 1597. However, it only covers a period of a week. When the mortality over the following weeks and a wider area is considered, the figures are much higher, giving an estimate of over 4000 deaths. Even this may be an underestimate because the government set an arbitrary cut-off date for the official figures.

References

Ackroyd, P. (2000) *London: the Biography*, London, Chatto and Windus.

Ash, C., Jasny, B. R., Roberts, L., Stone, R. and Sugden, A. M. (2008) 'Introduction to reimagining cities', *Science*, vol. 319, p. 739.

Brimblecombe, P. (1987) *The Big Smoke: A History of Air Pollution in London Since Medieval Times*, London, Methuen.

CIBSE (1998) *The Quest for Comfort*, London, Chartered Institution of Building Services Engineers.

Collins (1979) *Dictionary of the English Language*, London and Glasgow, Collins.

Davidson, C. (1982) *A Woman's Work is Never Done: A History of Housework in the British Isles 1650–1950*, London, Chatto and Windus.

Fouquet, R. (2008) *Heat, Power and Light: Revolutions in Energy Services*, Cheltenham, Edward Elgar Publishing.

Girardet, H. (1999) *Creating Sustainable Cities* (Schumacher Briefing No. 2), Totnes, Green Books/Schumacher Society.

GLA (2002) *50 Years On: The Struggle for Air Quality in London Since the Great Smog of December 1952*, Greater London Authority, http://www.london.gov.uk/mayor/environment/air_quality/docs/50_years_on.pdf (Accessed 12 October 2009).

Halliday, S. (1999) *The Great Stink of London: Sir Joseph Bazalgette and the Cleansing of the Victorian Metropolis*, Stroud, Sutton Publishing.

Johnson, S. (2006) *The Ghost Map*, London, Penguin.

Melville, C. (2006) 'London: the strength of a soft city', *Q-News*, issue 367.

Nansen, F. (1898) *Farthest North: Being the Record of a Voyage of Exploration of the Ship 'Fram' and of a Fifteen Months Sleigh Journey by Dr. Nansen and Lieut. Johansen etc.*, New York, London, Harper & Brothers 1898 (Accessed from Google).

Rogers, R. (1998) *Cities for a Small Planet*, London, Faber and Faber.

United Nations Populations Fund (2007) *State of World Population*, New York, United Nations Population Fund, p. 55.

White, H. P. (1963) *A Regional History of the Railways of Great Britain: Volume III, Greater London*, London, Phoenix House.

WWF (2006) *Ecological budget UK, Counting consumption, CO2 emissions, material flows and Ecological Footprint of the UK by regional devolved county*, Godalming, Surrey, World Wide Fund for Nature-UK, pp. 14,15.

Part 2

A low-carbon future for London?

Godfrey Boyle

Introduction

1

Ken Livingstone, Mayor of London, 2000–2008

It is almost impossible to exaggerate the danger of climate change. I have no doubt that it is the single biggest threat to the future development of human civilisation […] The aim of this plan is to deliver decisive action in London with the urgency that is required.

(Livingstone, 2007)

Nicky Gavron, Deputy Mayor of London, 2005–2008

…[m]ost of the world's cities, including London, are growing rapidly. Already cities consume three quarters of the world's energy and are responsible for eighty percent of all carbon emissions. […] London, as the pre-eminent world city, has a prime responsibility to act. And we are acting. […] through our planning policies […] we are spearheading a decentralised energy revolution here in London.

(Gavron, 2007)

Boris Johnson, Mayor of London, 2008–

Cities across the world share the common threat of climate change, and cities create most of the carbon emissions that are causing it, so it is vital we continue to work together to accelerate action on this issue.

(C40Cities, 2008)

Figure 2.1 shows two different energy supply strategies. The decentralised approach is a key component of London's energy policy.

■ Natural gas network
■ Central power station
■ Waste heat
■ Energy centre
■ Centralised system - bottom right
■ Decentralised system - top left
= Heat network
— Electricity network
— Gas network

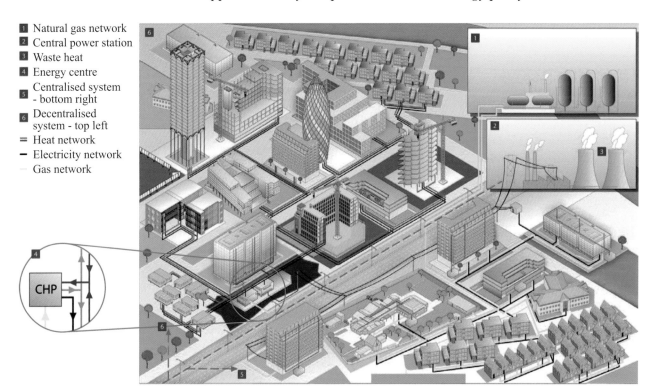

Figure 2.1 The centralised approach to supplying energy contrasted with a decentralised approach. In a centralised system electricity is transmitted from large power stations over long distances to supply buildings in the city. Natural gas is also pumped from far away to the city, where it is used in boilers within buildings to provide heat. In a decentralised system natural gas from distant sources (or, in the future, from more local sources) is supplied to combined heat and power (CHP) plant, and these in turn supply both electricity and heat to buildings in the surrounding area. The heat network is the flow and return of hot water. *(Source: London First, 2008)*

In Part 1 of this block we saw how some of London's major environmental problems of the past, such as the 'Great Stink' and the city's notorious smogs – problems that many perceived as intractable at the time – were eventually largely solved through a mixture of persistence, legislation, ingenuity and substantial capital expenditure.

In this second part I shall be looking in detail at another major environmental problem affecting cities, the urgency of which has become widely appreciated only in recent years, namely the threat of human-induced global climate change. This is likely to have very serious adverse implications for London and many other major cities around the world, and I shall examine what London and other world cities are doing to address the problem. You have already studied the greenhouse effect and its link to climate change and emissions of greenhouse gases in Block 1, but as a reminder, a brief list of some key milestones that have marked progress in the scientific, public and political recognition of the climate change issue are given in Box 2.1.

Box 2.1   Some world and UK milestones in scientific, public and political recognition of the climate change issue

1958	Charles Keeling begins accurate measurements of atmospheric CO_2 concentrations at Mauna Loa, Hawaii, leading to awareness of rising levels
1988	NASA scientist James Hansen addresses US Congress, asserting with very high certainty that global warming is occurring and that human greenhouse gas emissions are the main cause
1988	UK Prime Minister Margaret Thatcher warns the Royal Society that '...we have unwittingly begun an experiment with the system of the planet itself'
1989	Intergovernmental Panel on Climate Change (IPCC) formed
1990	IPCC's First Assessment warns of seriousness of climate change
1992	United Nations Framework Convention on Climate Change (UNFCCC) formed at United Nations 'Earth Summit' in Rio de Janeiro
1995	IPCC's Second Assessment: 'The balance of evidence suggests a discernible human influence on global climate'
1997	Kyoto Protocol: Majority of nations agree to make cuts in CO_2 emissions by 2008–2012 (levels of cuts vary). But does not become international law until 2005, when required number of nations become signatories
2000	UK Royal Commission on Environmental Pollution proposes a 60% cut in UK CO_2 emissions by 2050 and concludes: 'The enormous challenge posed by humanity's intervention in Earth's climate, threatening generations to come, demands action [...]'
2000	UK Government publishes *Climate Change: the UK Programme* setting out an effective framework of action to reduce the UK's emissions, and aiming to put the UK on a clearer path to a low-carbon economy.
2001	IPPC Third Assessment: 'There is new and stronger evidence that most of the warming observed over the last 50 years is attributable to human activities'
2006	The UK Treasury's 'Stern Report' (Stern, 2006) warns that delayed action over climate change will be much more costly in the long term than more prompt action
2007	IPCC Fourth Assessment Report: 'Human-induced warming of the climate system is widespread'
2008	European Union agrees a 20% cut in CO_2 emissions by 2020, to be increased to 30% if other non-EU countries agree similar measures
2008	UK Committee on Climate Change proposes that the UK should adopt a series of reducing, legally binding 5-year 'carbon budgets', aiming to cut CO_2 emissions by 80% by 2050
2009	UK Government White Paper on Climate Change accepts Climate Committee's recommendations and proposes a wide range of measures aimed at achieving 80% cuts by 2050
2009	Copenhagen conference aims to agree further worldwide CO_2 reductions to follow the end of the Kyoto agreement in 2011

Firstly I'll take an initial look at some of the actions that London is taking to tackle climate change, introduced by a video on the course DVD.

Then, coming back to this text, I'll examine in more detail London's greenhouse gas emission levels and what the city proposes to do to mitigate (i.e. reduce) these emissions. I shall examine the *London Mayor's Energy Strategy*, published in 2004, and *The Mayor's Climate Change Action Plan*, launched in 2007. These show how the Greater London Authority (GLA) proposes to reduce London's CO_2 emissions in the main sectors of the city's economy (the domestic, commercial and public, industry and transport sectors) and to shift the city's energy supplies towards more efficient and low-emission systems.

I'll also discuss the strategy's progress to date and its prospects for success in coming decades.

Then, with the help of another video, you'll take a look at the role of political leadership in enabling the changes that will be required to mitigate carbon emissions in London.

Lastly, you'll move beyond London to look briefly at a much wider initiative, led by London, to work with other world cities such as New York to achieve similar major reductions in the greenhouse gas emissions of cities over coming decades.

Finally, it is worth stressing at the outset that the story of London's initiatives to mitigate climate change is a fast-moving one: it will probably have changed significantly by the time you read this. If you would like to keep up with the latest developments, you can check the website of the Greater London Authority and some of the other relevant sites available via the links on the course website.

Cities, sustainability and climate change

2

At some time during the early years of the twenty-first century it is estimated that, for the first time in human history, the majority of the world's population will be living in cities. If this trend towards increasing urbanisation continues, as seems likely, it is estimated that by 2050 approximately 70% of the human population will be city-based (United Nations, 2007). This remarkable global shift from rural to urban living implies that solutions to the problems of environmental and social sustainability will increasingly need to focus on cities (see also *Science*, 2008, and Starke, 2007).

London is one of the world's leading business, financial and cultural centres and is the capital city of the United Kingdom. Greater London is the most populous municipality in the European Union, with a population in 2006 of 7.5 million (see Box 2.2).

In Block 1, Part 2, Section 3 described 'Climate change and the carbon connection'. In Activity 2.2 in that section you were asked to make notes on the impacts of global temperature rises, and Figure 2.16 summarised the impacts likely to be associated with rising global temperature.

The principal effects of climate change on London and similar major world cities, if mitigation and adaptation measures are not adopted and effective, are likely to be serious. They include:

- increased summer temperatures, leading to premature deaths among vulnerable populations
- increased extremes of rainfall, leading to excess surface run-off of water and local flooding
- rising sea levels, necessitating improved defences against flooding of low-lying areas.

Box 2.2   London

Figure 2.2 A scene of London showing the old and the new: the Tower of London (right foreground) and 'The Gherkin' (actually called the Swiss Re building) now one of the tallest buildings in the City of London.

London is the de facto capital of the United Kingdom. It has been an influential city for two millennia and its history goes back to its founding by the Romans. The city's core, the ancient City of London, still retains its limited medieval boundaries. However, since at least the nineteenth century, the name 'London' has also referred to the whole metropolis that has developed around it. Today the bulk of this conurbation forms the London metropolitan region and the Greater London administrative area, with its own elected mayor and assembly.

London is one of the world's foremost global cities, alongside New York City and one of the largest financial centres, alongside New York City and Tokyo. Central London is home to the headquarters of more than half of the UK's top 100 listed companies (the FTSE 100) and more than 100 of Europe's 500 largest. The city's influence in politics, education, entertainment, media, fashion, the arts and culture in general contributes to its global position. It is a major tourist destination for both domestic and overseas visitors. London hosted the 1908 and 1948 Summer Olympics and will host the 2012 Summer Olympics.

London has a wide range of peoples, cultures, and religions, and more than 300 languages are spoken within the city. In July 2007, it had an official population of 7,556,900 within the boundaries of Greater London, making it the most populous municipality in the European Union. The Greater London Urban Area (the second largest in the EU) has a population of 8,278,251, while the metropolitan area (the largest in the EU) has an estimated total population of between 12 million and 14 million. The public transport network, administered by Transport for London, is the most extensive in the world. London Heathrow Airport is the world's busiest airport by number of international passengers and the airspace is the busiest of any city in the world.

(Source: adapted from Wikipedia, 2009)

2.1   London: towards a zero-carbon future?

You should now view the video *London: towards a zero-carbon future?* on the course DVD, which is approximately 10 minutes long. It describes London's climate change initiatives, was filmed in 2006, and includes the following participants:

Allan Jones, former Chief Executive Officer of the London Climate Change Agency (LCCA)*

Ashok Sinha of the London-based pressure group Stop Climate Chaos

Mark Watts, climate change adviser to the former Mayor of London, Ken Livingstone

Miles Hearn of the London Energy Services Company (ESCO).

When you have viewed the video, read the discussion and then attempt SAQ 2.1.

* The London Climate Change Agency is now incorporated into the London Development Agency – one of the organisational changes introduced following the election of Boris Johnson as London Mayor in 2008.

2.1.1   Discussion

The video looks at the carbon emission reduction initiatives being encouraged and implemented by the GLA. If London can radically reduce its carbon footprint, the GLA hopes it will set an example for urban environments across the world.

As the first interviewee, Allan Jones, points out, the world's cities are responsible for 70 per cent of the world's CO_2 emissions, they are most at risk from climate change, they are a major cause of climate change, and they are very well placed to tackle the problem.

The importance of tackling the threat of climate change is underlined by Ashok Sinha. The warning signs, he says, are clear, and the UK needs to 'get real' about developing renewable and sustainable energy.

London consumes as much energy as Greece, and as Mark Watts observes:

If London is able to show that it's possible to have a low-carbon or even a zero-carbon future, then other cities around the world, and indeed, maybe governments, will recognise that this isn't a fantasy […] it's possible to have a successful economy, a vibrant city, and yet be low carbon.

Some pioneering developments in and around London have pointed the way, as the video briefly shows. These include the Beddington Zero Energy Development (BedZED) in the London Borough of Sutton (mentioned in Block 1), which is designed to produce as much energy annually from renewables as it consumes, and the Borough of Woking, near London, which has cut the CO_2 emissions from its council buildings by more than 70% since 1990, mainly using *combined heat and power (CHP)* plants, connected via its own private distribution networks.

The Woking scheme was headed by Allan Jones, who was then recruited by the London mayor in 2004 to achieve similar results on a much larger scale in the capital by leading the LCCA. One of the aims of the agency was to demonstrate that climate-friendly solutions can be commercially viable. As Mark Watts observes:

> We wanted to demonstrate to the private sector that delivering decentralised energy was both efficient and economic – and, indeed, that the private sector could make a profit out of it.

In order to do so, amongst other things the LCCA created a joint venture company with the major energy supplier EDF Energy. EDF is the majority shareholder in the 'London Energy Services Company', or 'London ESCO', with the LCCA as minority shareholder. EDF is already a major supplier of electricity and gas to London. Its parent company is the huge French state-owned electricity utility Electricité de France. As Miles Hearn points out, the company's initial aim is to implement those 40 or so decentralised energy projects which it estimates will have the greatest impact on reducing London's carbon emissions. He describes one of these projects that is already in operation: the Barkantine CHP project shown in the video, which supplies heat and electricity to some 500 homes in the London borough of Tower Hamlets, reducing CO_2 emissions by about 2 tonnes per resident.

Under the London mayor's Energy Strategy (described in more detail in Section 3) the mayor requires that all new buildings over a certain size, if they are to be granted planning permission, must be designed in as energy-efficient a way as possible and must consider adopting CHP wherever feasible. Developers are also required to supply at least 10% of the building's energy from renewables – and this figure is being raised to 20%. As Mark Watts emphasises, 'the only new developments that are going to happen in London, where the mayor has any power over them, are going to be low and zero-carbon developments, we are simply not going to allow anything else to be built in London of any scale'.

The GLA is aiming to set a good example in its own buildings, such as the Palestra, headquarters of the LCCA and the London Development Agency, which has a photovoltaic array on its roof, and the City Hall, where a photovoltaic array has also been installed.

Renewable energy systems are also being installed on a larger scale. In the London borough of Dagenham two large wind turbines provide enough power for 1200 homes, and in the Thames estuary just outside London, as Allan Jones observes, the world's largest offshore wind farm, the 1000 MW London Array, will soon be built. (The first phase of this project was given the green light in May 2009; completion is scheduled for 2012, in time for the London Olympics.)

Mark Watts also points to London's initiatives in reducing transport energy emissions. As the video shows, three experimental low-emission, fuel-cell-powered buses fuelled by hydrogen are running in central London, with more to follow. At present, the hydrogen is produced by 're-forming' natural gas, but Allan Jones hopes that eventually these will be powered by a hydrogen-rich gas produced by 'gasifying' a proportion of London's residual (post-recycling) wastes instead of incinerating or landfilling them.

In order to make these moves towards a low-carbon city a reality, public awareness and support is essential. Fortunately, as Mark Watts points out, opinion polls show that 95% of Londoners recognise that climate change is a serious problem, and it is one of the top four or five topics they are most concerned about.

As Ashok Sinha observes, public awareness of renewable and sustainable energy has increased markedly in recent years: it has moved from the fringe to the mainstream. Moreover, moving to a renewably powered energy system is technologically feasible:

> It's well established that there is enough natural resource out there to meet our energy needs many times over. The issue here in the end is whether […] we are prepared to put the [political] resource behind it and whether we are also prepared to address the changes to our lifestyles that will be necessary so that we are not profligate in our use of energy.

Mark Watts concludes the video on an optimistic note:

> A zero-carbon future is a positive future; it's not something where we are going to have to reduce quality of life [or] standard of living for people – it's one where people's quality of life will improve.

SAQ 2.1   Promoting efficient decentralised energy systems

Make a preliminary list of the measures mentioned in the DVD that the Greater London Authority and its associated organisations are employing to promote more efficient, decentralised energy systems. Which of these measures directly involve action by individual householders, which involve action by companies and organisations, and which entail action by local or central government?

3   Reducing London's carbon emissions

3.1   Energy use and carbon emissions in London

Residents of cities, like the residents of rural settlements, contribute to climate change through the emissions of carbon dioxide (CO_2) and the other greenhouse gases they generate, mainly as a result of their use of carbon-based fossil fuels. However, energy use in cities is often more efficient than in rural areas: housing density is higher, leading to lower energy per unit of floor area; transport distances are shorter; and there is better provision of public transport, which is more energy efficient than private vehicle use. These factors can help lower the per capita greenhouse gas emissions of city dwellers.

Figure 1.34 in Part 1 illustrated London's energy use between 1950 and 2000, and showed the changing mix of fuels, with 'clean' natural gas supplanting solid fuels from the 1970s. Natural gas combustion produces lower CO_2 emissions per unit of useful energy than burning solid fossil fuel.

During the 1990s, as shown in Figure 2.3(a), carbon dioxide emissions from fossil fuel use in London reduced slightly, from about 45 million tonnes of CO_2 in 1991 to about 42 million tonnes in 1999. They then rose slightly, to around 44 million tonnes in 2006 (excluding emissions from aviation). The distribution of emissions between the different sectors of London's economy in 2006 is shown in Figure 2.3(b).

It is worth noting, however, that these emission figures do not include CO_2 emissions from international travel by UK residents, or those 'embedded' in products manufactured abroad and imported to the UK for use in London. For the UK as a whole, it is estimated that such embedded emissions could add nearly 40% to the total, and for London the additional percentage is probably similar. According to government estimates (DEFRA, 2008) CO_2 emissions within the UK in 2004 were approximately 540 million tonnes; but emissions associated with UK consumption, including emissions from international travel and the production and transportation of imported goods (but excluding emissions from the production of goods for UK export) were approximately 750 million tonnes, some 39% higher.

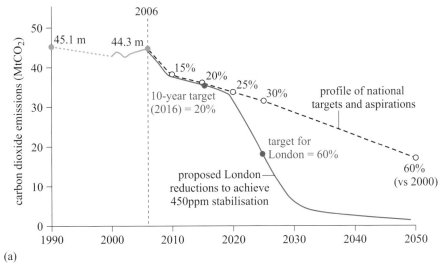

(a)

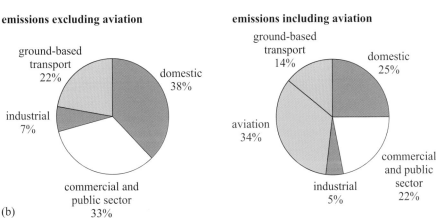

(b)

Figure 2.3 London's emissions: (a) carbon emissions 1990–2006 and projections to 2050 compared with UK national government projections; (b) CO$_2$ emissions in 2006 by sector, including and excluding aviation. If aviation is excluded the domestic sector is the largest, followed by the commercial and public sector, then ground-based transport and finally the industrial sector. The aviation contribution increases the total level of emissions to 67 million tonnes; it includes fuel used by aircraft taking off and landing at London's Heathrow and City airports (Gatwick, Stansted and Luton airports are outside the GLA boundary). *(Source: redrawn from GLA, 2007)*

3.2   The mayor's energy and climate change strategies

In the *Mayor's Energy Strategy* (GLA, 2004), the GLA proposed ambitious plans to achieve major reductions in London's energy use and energy-related carbon emissions. Central to the strategy was the deployment of decentralised energy systems, in the form of high-efficiency *combined cooling, heating and power* (CCHP) systems, together with renewable energy sources such as solar and wind power (see Figure 2.1). CCHP involves capturing the 'waste' heat from locally based electricity generating systems and putting it to use in heating and/or cooling nearby buildings. (See Box 2.3).

Box 2.3   Explaining CHP and CCHP

Traditionally, in the UK, power stations have been seen as making only electricity, yet the generation process produces very large amounts of low-temperature waste heat. […] About a third of the UK's delivered energy is used for space and water heating, i.e. at final use temperatures of less than 60°C. Combined heat and power (CHP or 'co- generation') plants produce both electricity and heat at a sufficiently high temperature to be useful. This can enable them to achieve a high overall thermal efficiency.

[…]

Outside the large industrial plant, CHP takes two forms. Small-scale CHP essentially takes the power station to the user, usually in the form of a small reciprocating engine similar to a car or truck engine, but running on natural gas as a fuel. This will drive an electrical generator typically with a power rating between 100 kW and 1 MW output.

In the UK there are hundreds of institutions, especially hospitals, community centres and large hotels, which have a sufficiently large year-round demand for both electricity and heat to warrant investing in their own CHP plant. Although a small-scale CHP unit may only have an electricity generation efficiency of about 30%, less than that of a conventional power station, the ability to use the waste heat makes it more energy efficient overall. This kind of comparison can be expressed in a Sankey diagram, which is a flow chart showing the overall energy inputs and outputs of a system. The [top] half of Figure [2.4] shows the energy flows for a conventional power station […] . The [bottom] half shows the energy flows for a small-scale CHP unit, including the use of waste heat. The actual amount of waste heat that can be used depends on the temperature at which it is required, but for typical heating applications the overall thermal efficiency can be over 80%. Such schemes have been extensively encouraged in the UK since the mid-1980s and are widely used in countries such as the Netherlands and Denmark.

(Everett, 2003)

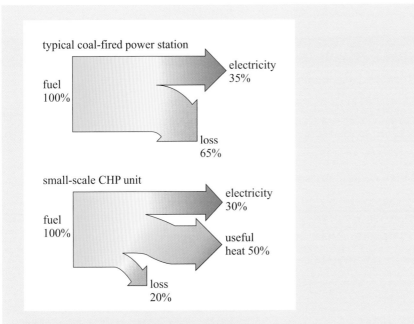

**Figure 2.4 'Sankey diagrams' comparing a
conventional power station and a small CHP plant**

The 'waste' heat from a CHP plant can also be used if necessary
for cooling in buildings. In these 'combined cooling, heating and
power' (CCHP) systems (also known as 'tri-generation' systems)
the heat is used to drive an absorption-type refrigeration system,
similar to those commonly used in caravans or 'recreational
vehicles' and powered by a butane gas burner.

A key aim of the strategy was for London to double its installed CCHP
capacity by 2010, compared with 2000. The strategy also envisaged the
deployment by 2010 of 25 000 solar water heating systems, 7000 solar
photovoltaic roofs, 500 small wind turbines and six large wind turbines.
All 32 London boroughs (the sub-units of local government in London)
should have at least one 'zero-carbon' development (i.e. one having zero
net carbon emissions, measured annually) and were urged to implement
targets for renewable energy deployment. All major developments over
1000 square metres in floor area would need to be approved by the
mayor. To gain approval they would need to incorporate energy-/carbon-
saving measures such as *passive solar design* and natural ventilation,
and should utilise CCHP and renewable energy wherever possible. The
aim was for renewables to supply enough electricity for 100 000 homes
and heat for 10 000 homes by 2010. These targets were to be tripled
by 2020.

Box 2.4 explains some key terms in renewable energy.

Box 2.4   Renewable energy: some key terms explained

Passive solar space heating

Design of buildings so that energy from the Sun is captured and retained to warm the interior, e.g. by using glass roofs to allow solar radiation to enter the building, and heavy materials to retain captured solar heat.

Solar water heating

Using energy from the Sun to heat water, e.g. in a circulating system in which water passes through a blackened panel covered by a transparent panel that faces the Sun.

Solar photovoltaics

Solar panels that convert energy from the Sun directly into electricity.

Biofuels

Fuels derived from biological material, usually plants or animal wastes (excluding fossil fuels, which are derived from long-dead biological material).

Ground-source heat pump

A *ground-source heat pump* is a system that takes advantage of heat retention in the soil and extracts it via a network of buried pipes and a refrigerator-like pump that raises its temperature.

The GLA has encouraged the installation of a number of demonstration renewable energy schemes, for example using photovoltaic arrays and wind turbines, at various locations around London. And in addition to encouraging measures to be implemented within Greater London, as mentioned in the video, it has supported ambitious plans to site several major offshore wind farms in the estuary of the River Thames, downstream from London – though this area is just outside the Authority's jurisdiction. These include the 1000 MW London Array, the 500 MW Greater Gabbard Array and the 300 MW Thanet Array (see Figure 2.5). The London Array is scheduled for completion in 2012 and the other two in 2011. Together they should supply the domestic electricity needs of a quarter of London's households.

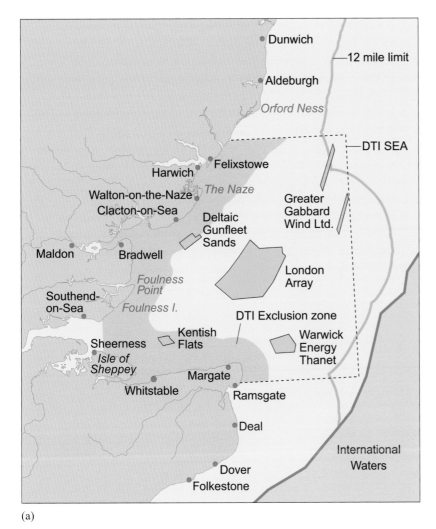

(a)

(b)

Figure 2.5 **(a) Locations of the proposed offshore wind farms in the Thames estuary: the London Array, the Greater Gabbard Array, the Thanet Array and the Gunfleet Sands Array; (b) the existing offshore wind farm at Kentish Flats. DTI is the Department of Trade and Industry (now Department of Business, Industry and Skills (BIS)). SEA stands for Strategic Environmental Assessment area.**

The Mayor's Energy Strategy and the initiatives mentioned above laid the groundwork for *The Mayor's Climate Change Action Plan*, published in 2007 (GLA, 2007). The plan's main aim was ambitious: to achieve a 20% reduction in London's CO_2 emissions by 2016 and a 60% reduction by 2025, compared with emissions in 1990 (Figures 2.6 and 2.3a). This aim, when announced, was more challenging than the UK government's target of 60% by 2050 – though the government's 2050 target was subsequently raised to 80% on the recommendation of the government's Committee on Climate Change, set up as part of the Climate Change Act 2008. The committee also recommended in late 2008 that the UK should have an interim target of a 34% reduction in emissions by 2020, compared with 1990 levels (Committee on Climate Change, 2008). In July 2009 the UK government published its *UK Low Carbon Transition Plan* (DECC, 2009a) setting out its 'National Strategy for Climate and Energy' and showing how it proposes to achieve the 34% by 2020 target recommended by the Climate Committee.

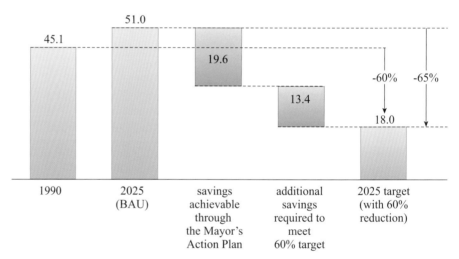

Figure 2.6 Estimated CO_2 savings achievable by 2025 through the *Mayor's Climate Change Action Plan* and additional savings required to meet a 60% reduction target. Units are million tonnes of CO_2 (the national UK target has been raised to 80%, see text), BAU is 'Business as usual'. *(Source: redrawn from GLA, 2007)*

As can be seen from Figures 2.6 and 2.7, London's CO_2 emissions in a 'business as usual' scenario (i.e. in the absence of any actions to reduce CO_2 emissions) would rise from 45 million tonnes in 1990 to 51 million tonnes in 2025. It is estimated that the various measures in the Action Plan should reduce emissions by 19.6 million tonnes by 2025. Additional actions by UK national government would be required to enable a further reduction of 13 million tonnes, enabling the target 60% reduction to be achieved.

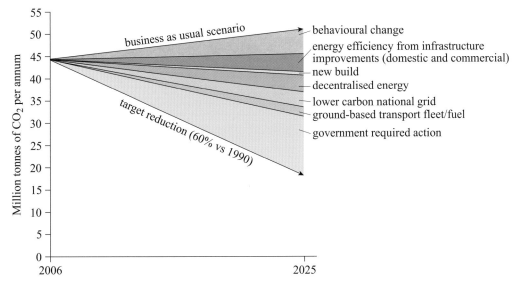

Figure 2.7 Estimated contributions over time of various measures to achieving London's CO$_2$ reduction target for 2025, compared with 'business as usual' *(Source: redrawn from GLA, 2007)*

SAQ 2.2   Wedges: the pros and cons

You may have noticed the similarity of Figure 2.7 to Pacala and Socolow's CO$_2$ reduction 'wedges' which you encountered in Block 1, Part 4, Section 2.

What is the main difference between the Pacala/Socolow wedges and those shown in Figure 2.7? Can you list the 'pros' and 'cons' of this wedges approach?

3.3   Key aspects of the *Climate Change Action Plan*

One of the key measures proposed by the GLA to mitigate emissions of greenhouse gases (principally CO$_2$) included, as you have seen, the establishment of a London Climate Change Agency (LCCA) to implement the strategy. The LCCA, as mentioned in the DVD, in turn set up a London Energy Supply Company (ESCO), in partnership with the major electricity utility EDF Energy, to roll out CCHP and other decentralised energy schemes across the capital during the coming decade and beyond. (The LCCA, as noted above, has now been incorporated into the London Development Agency and it is no longer a separate entity. Most of its work, however, continues).

Another key measure was the use of the mayor's planning powers of scrutiny over all major new building developments. These are being used to reduce CO$_2$ emissions from new buildings. They involve a three-stage approach to reducing energy use and CO_2 emissions, summarised in the slogan 'Be Lean, Be Clean, and Be Green':

* *Be Lean: Use Less Energy*. This involves implementing stringent energy conservation measures.
* *Be Clean: Use Energy Efficiently*. This involves using combined cooling, heating and power (CCHP) and other energy-efficient technologies wherever possible.
* *Be Green: Use Renewable Energy*. This involves supplying a significant proportion (10–20%) of the energy demand from renewable sources.

In practice, this hierarchy of measures is interpreted flexibly by planners, according to the constraints of each individual project.

3.4 Reducing CO_2 emissions in the domestic, commercial and public sectors

In the domestic sector, the actions proposed in the Action Plan involve establishing a 'Green Homes Programme', including an energy and greenhouse emissions awareness campaign and a one-stop advice service, and making available subsidised insulation for home owners, particularly those on lower incomes. For those householders who can afford to pay, a 'Green Concierge Service' has been set up, offering energy and emissions audits with recommended measures to reduce emissions, and a project management service to facilitate their implementation.

For the commercial and public sectors the LCCA has established a 'Green Organisations Programme'. This includes a 'Better Buildings Partnership' between the LCCA and major building owners, and a 'Green 500' badging scheme for organisations, to encourage emission-reducing behaviour changes and improved operations by building occupants and managers.

The Green 500 scheme now (2009) has 154 large businesses and public sector members, each of which receives a carbon assessment, is helped to develop an emissions reduction plan and commits to publish its progress annually. Businesses are offered a 'carbon mentor' to work with them to help implement the plan and achieve their target. There are annual awards to recognise those that reach their target and for top achievers.

The Better Building Partnership (BBP) has 11 members representing London's leading commercial property companies, which work together with occupiers to develop energy-efficiency programmes for London's existing building stock. It has set a target to cut 500 000 tonnes of CO_2 emissions by 2012. The BBP aims to retrofit buildings with energy-efficient measures. These include updating boiler controls, converting to energy-efficient lighting, more efficient heating systems, improved insulation and solar water heating.

3.5 Reducing CO$_2$ emissions in the new buildings and energy supply sectors

New buildings in London are only a small proportion of the total building stock, most of which is old. As already mentioned, planning applications for major new developments require the scrutiny and approval of the mayor. To what extent has this process been successful? Professor Tony Day (whose views you will encounter in Section 4) and his colleagues at London's South Bank University studied a sample of 113 such applications, out of 350 made in 2004–6. Their main conclusion was that GLA policies are likely to lead to savings of roughly one million tonnes of CO$_2$ per year by 2010 in new buildings. Approximately a quarter of these savings are from renewables; the rest is from CCHP and improved energy efficiency. The renewables contribution was small when the policy was first introduced, but a 10% contribution is now routinely achieved and the renewables target has been raised to 20% (Day et al., 2009).

For new buildings the GLA also proposed revisions to the London Plan to encourage further use of decentralised energy, together with improvements in advice and support to building developers and to the staff in the 32 London boroughs responsible for building control and for granting planning permission for smaller developments. It also proposed funding exemplary low- and zero-carbon developments by the London Development Agency (LDA) – such as the 2012 Olympic Village and projects in the London boroughs like the Beddington Zero Energy Development (BedZED) in the Borough of Sutton that was depicted in Block 1.

In the energy supply sector, the Action Plan measures include encouragement for major increases in the use of combined heat and power (CHP) and, where appropriate, combined cooling, heating and power (CCHP). They also encourage generation of energy from waste and the use of on-site renewable energy sources, such as passive solar space heating, solar water heating, solar photovoltaics (Figure 2.8), biofuels, ground-source heat pumps, building-integrated wind turbines – and large-scale renewable energy projects located near London, such as the offshore wind farms in the Thames estuary.

Figure 2.8 Solar photovoltaic roof on City Hall, the GLA's headquarters

3.6   Reducing CO_2 emissions in ground-based transport

Ground-based transport in London comprises cars, lorries, buses, bicycles, taxis, rail and the London Underground system. The Action Plan's measures here include major investments to improve the efficiency of the public transport system: more efficient vehicle operation; promoting low-carbon vehicles and fuels; introducing carbon pricing for transport.

Prior to the publication of the Action Plan, various other measures to cut London's transport emissions and reduce traffic congestion had already been introduced. These included the introduction of congestion charging, involving a payment by motorists of £8 per day to drive into the city centre. Low- and zero-emission vehicles are exempt from the charge. As a result, traffic levels in central London have decreased by about 15%. The proceeds of the congestion charge have been used to fund a shift to public transport, involving many more and newer buses, improvements to the rail and underground network, and better facilities for cycling and walking.

Other transport-related measures include requiring London Underground (which uses about 3% of the city's electricity) to buy power from renewable energy suppliers and introducing a 'Low Emission Zone' in which it is mandatory for large vehicles entering the Greater London area to meet strict emission standards. The GLA also aims to convert all 8000 London buses to lower-emission 'hybrids' (with combined diesel–electric engines). It is also supporting the London Hydrogen Partnership, which has initially introduced three 'zero-emission' fuel cell/hydrogen-powered buses into regular service, as part of an EU demonstration project to test the technology and introduce it to the public (Figure 2.9).

Figure 2.9 London bus powered by hydrogen. The hydrogen powers a fuel cell that in turn generates electricity to drive the bus's electric motor. The hydrogen at present is produced by re-forming' natural gas, a fossil fuel, but the GLA envisages hydrogen supplies ultimately being produced from waste or other renewable sources. (The first three hydrogen buses have been temporarily withdrawn, since the EU demonstration project of which they were a part has come to an end. However, the GLA plans to introduce another 10 hydrogen-fuelled buses in 2010)

Boris Johnson, the current London mayor, is a keen cyclist. One of the key policies he has promoted since being elected in 2008 involves the introduction of a city-wide bicycle hire scheme, similar to that in Paris. Another new policy involves the promotion of electric vehicles (cars, taxis, vans, etc.) in the capital (GLA, 2009).

SAQ 2.3   Behavioural and technological changes

Two approaches to reducing the CO_2 emissions of London's transport system, (a) the bicycle hire scheme and (b) increasing the use of electric vehicles, both involve combinations of technological change and changes in people's behaviour.

Describe briefly the behavioural and technological changes that are involved in each, and their relative importance.

Can you think of a CO_2 emission reduction measure in the transport field that involves behavioural change only, with no technological changes?

3.7   The Climate Change Action Plan – how successful?

If enacted in full, the measures in the London Climate Change Action Plan should enable CO_2 emissions to be reduced by about 27% by 2025. But in the GLA's view this is not enough – a reduction of at least 60% by 2025 is needed if London is to contribute its share of the global CO_2 reductions needed to stabilise climate. To get to 60%, additional national government action is required. In the GLA's view this involves setting a firm price for carbon emissions, and removing regulatory obstacles to deploying CCHP and renewables.

This is beginning to happen: the UK government in 2008 provided new encouragement for decentralised energy in its Climate and Energy Bills. It agreed in principle to create a 'feed-in tariff' offering increased prices for decentralised electricity sold to the National Grid, similar to Germany's highly successful model, and to introduce a similar scheme in which premium prices would be paid for heat production from renewables. In July 2009 the government issued a consultation document (DECC, 2009b) setting forth detailed proposals for an electricity feed-in tariff (to be called the 'Clean Energy Cash Back' scheme) to come into effect in 2010, and a similar 'Renewable Heat Obligation' to be introduced in 2011.

Progress in reducing London's emissions has so far been modest, though as we have seen, a reduction of one million tonnes per year in CO_2 emissions from new buildings is likely to have been achieved by 2010. But it is probably too early to judge the long-term success of the GLA's plans – especially if they are subject to significant changes under the new post-2008 political leadership.

The London Assembly is the body of elected members whose main role is to scrutinise the work of the Greater London Authority in general and the mayor in particular. In 2009 the Assembly's Budget and Performance Committee issued a report on the GLA's environment spending plans and priorities that was critical of developments under Boris Johnson's new, post-2008 administration. It concluded:

> We find that there is much desirable work happening but that there is a shortage of strategic leadership. By this we mean that although the GLA is corporately committed to long-term targets, particularly of CO_2 emission reductions but also, for example, for air quality, the selection and prioritisation and monitoring of projects does not appear to be driven from City Hall towards the achievement of those targets. [...]
>
> As an example, the bicycle hire project, which accounts for about a quarter of proposed environment spend, and over 80 per cent of the increase in budget for this year, appears as yet to offer no targets and fit no strategic plan towards environmental mitigation or improvement. [...] As another example, were it not for an additional allocation of funds since January this year by the London Development Agency, there would have been a cut in programmes to tackle climate change. This seems odd given the declared priority of such works. And we question whether proposed staffing cuts, in the environment team, will further reduce City Hall's ability to lead on and coordinate in this area.

(London Assembly, 2009)

In addition to possible political changes under the new GLA regime, further problems in implementing CO_2 reductions in London are likely to include the very large scale of the investment required – hundreds of millions of pounds per year. This represents a formidable challenge, especially in view of the 'credit crunch' that (at the time of writing, September 2009) is inhibiting investment in many large-scale projects around the world. National, and possibly international, government action could well be needed to galvanise public and private investment on the scale that is required.

SAQ 2.4   Stages in recognising and solving environmental problems

In Part 1 you saw how in previous centuries two major environmental problems of London were eventually recognised and solved in stages. Can you recall those stages and identify the similar stages involved in tackling the climate change problems in London?

Summary of Sections 2 and 3

The video in Section 2 looked at some of the steps being taken by the GLA to reduce London's greenhouse gas emissions and introduced some of the key individuals involved. Section 3 looked in more detail at London's CO_2 emissions and at the various measures that the GLA is implementing to reduce them in the sectors of London's economy, as outlined in the mayor's climate change strategy. Finally, the prospects for success of the strategy and some criticisms that have been made of its implementation were considered.

The role of political leadership

4

In developing and implementing London's ambitious plans to mitigate climate change, the role of strong political leadership has been crucial. From the beginning of his term of office in 2000, London's first mayor, Ken Livingstone (Figure 2.10(a)), recognised the seriousness of the climate change problem, the need for London to take action – and the need for further supporting action at national and international governmental levels. As he later wrote in his foreword to *The Mayor's London Climate Change Action Plan*:

> It is almost impossible to exaggerate the danger of climate change. I have no doubt that it is the single biggest threat to the future development of human civilisation
>
> [...]
>
> The aim of this plan is to deliver decisive action in London with the urgency that is required.
>
> [...]
>
> This action plan demonstrates that London can make deep and meaningful cuts in its emissions through actions by London public authorities, by businesses, and by individual Londoners. For the next ten years we can meet the target reductions that scientists say are necessary.
>
> The difficult truth, however, is that without action at national and international level we cannot continue to achieve this through to 2025 and beyond.
>
> [...]
>
> That is why we have established the C40 – a forum of the largest cities in the world, in partnership with the Clinton Foundation, to accelerate emissions reductions among cities.

(Livingstone, 2007)

Livingstone's Deputy Mayor from 2005–8, Nicky Gavron (Figure 2.10(b)), who chaired the London Climate Change Agency, was equally emphatic, stressing the need for London to lead a revolution in energy production and use:

> ...[m]ost of the world's cities, including London, are growing rapidly. Already cities consume three quarters of the world's energy and are responsible for eighty percent of all carbon emissions. [...] London, as the pre-eminent world city, has a prime responsibility to act. And we are acting.

(a) Ken Livingstone was Mayor of London from 2000–2008. He was also Leader of the Greater London Council from 1981 until its abolition in 1986, and was Labour member of Parliament for Brent East from 1987–2000.

(b) Nicky Gavron was deputy mayor of London from 2004–2008 and Chair of the London Climate Change Agency. She continues as a Labour member of the London Assembly.

(c) Boris Johnson was elected Mayor of London in 2008. Previously he was editor of the *Spectator* magazine and Conservative member of Parliament for Henley-on-Thames.

Figure 2.10 (a) Ken Livingstone; (b) Nicky Gavron; (c) Boris Johnson

[…] [t]hrough our planning policies and the London Climate Change Agency we are spearheading a decentralised energy revolution here in London. Remote centralised power stations are the primary cause of climate change: they waste their heat and lose power through national grid transmission. Our solution is to decentralise power, generating it locally so the heat can be used to warm and cool our buildings. […]

… [w]e are introducing policies and projects which cut across those institutional boundaries which keep the big carbon producing sectors – energy, waste, transport and water – separate.

[…]

[But these] major planks of our action plan will only realise their full potential to cut carbon emissions if government removes the barriers currently holding back the roll-out of decentralised energy and the large-scale production of renewable gases and liquid fuels from waste.

(Gavron, 2007)

When Boris Johnson (Figure 2.10(c)) was elected Mayor of London in May 2008, replacing Livingstone, there was some uncertainty that the city's climate change policy leadership would continue. The misgivings of some environmentalists were strengthened when Johnson scrapped his predecessor's proposed extension of the congestion charging zone to the west of London, together with his proposal to raise the daily congestion charge to £25 for large 'gas-guzzling' vehicles – this had been aimed at raising funds for a London-wide bicycle hire scheme. However, more recent indications suggest that many of the GLA's original climate change policy goals will be retained – although the strategy for achieving them may change.

4.1   Analysing the mayor's speech

You should now view the four videos in the *Analysing the mayor's speech* section on the course DVD. The first video is of Boris Johnson's speech to the Environment Agency in November 2008, in which he gave details of his views on climate change and the environment generally. While viewing it, you should note what you consider to be the main points made by the mayor and also any questions or comments on the speech that you consider significant. This is followed by an analysis of the speech by three experts (in the remaining three videos):

John Vidal (the *Guardian*)

Samantha Heath (Chief Executive, London Sustainability Exchange), and

Professor Tony Day (London South Bank University).

When you have viewed the four videos, read the discussion and then attempt SAQ 2.5.

4.1.1   Discussion

The main points made in Boris Johnson's Environment Agency speech

Johnson begins by noting that some people argue, in a time of recession, that environmental considerations such as clean energy or recycling have to be set aside. Instead, Johnson joins others in calling for a 'Green New Deal'. This is a reference to the 'New Deal' implemented by President Franklin D. Roosevelt in the USA in the 1930s, which involved major public expenditure on public works to combat the economic effects of the Great Depression. A Green New Deal in today's time of recession would involve employment-creating public expenditure on 'green' projects such as energy conservation. Johnson admits that in the past he had been very critical of the 'religion' of climate change but since becoming mayor his mind has been changed by the weight of scientific evidence. And in any case, he adds, reducing pollution makes aesthetic and economic sense.

As part of his job as mayor, he authorises many new developments that include combined heat and power (CHP), which reduce pollution and save money. London, he stresses, is committed to supplying 25% of energy locally by 2025, and in its building energy-efficiency programme aims to retrofit energy-saving measures in 25% of public buildings. Using similar measures, small and medium enterprises (SMEs) could save £720 million in energy bills and expand their profit margins by 10–20%. Over the next four years the GLA will also spend £100 million on climate change programmes, including helping households to install insulation.

Waste, Johnson argues, should be regarded not as rubbish but as a resource. He goes on to say:

> London spends roughly £12 billion on energy, including heating, when properly managed waste could generate two-thirds of our […] domestic electricity […] Councils are spending millions every year to send it to landfill, at a time when landfill taxes are rising and space is diminishing. And I think that is completely crazy.

> Again, working with the boroughs, we believe there are fantastic opportunities to lift recycling off its currently feeble level of twenty per cent and, among other measures, we hope to introduce 'Recyclebank' to London, by which an American company will pay you the more you recycle.

> ... if we get these measures right and if we pursue them vigorously, we have the prospect not just of reducing your council tax bill but of reducing your energy bill as well. And we can use our transport and procurement budgets […] to expand this energy-saving and energy-producing technology and to make London the technological and financial centre of the new green revolution.

> Renewable energy in Germany generates 250 000 jobs, compared to 15 000 in this country. (If) you look […] at the talent that […] is in the process of being liberated from our financial sector by the recent convulsions, you can see there are opportunities there for a new industry and there is a market just about to sprout in this city and we intend to use our public procurement budgets to help to fertilise it.

(a) John Vidal is Environment Editor of the *Guardian*.

(b) Samantha Heath is Chief Executive of the London Sustainability Exchange and a former Labour member of London Assembly (2000–2004).

(c) Tony Day is Professor of Energy Engineering and director of the Centre for Efficient and Renewable Energy in Buildings(CEREB) at London South Bank University.

Figure 2.11 (a) John Vidal; (b) Samantha Heath; (c) Tony Day

We have public procurement budgets of about thirteen billion pounds, one in fifty Londoners is employed by a GLA institution. I want to use our influence as powerfully as possible to drive forward the electrification of the motor car. The GLA currently has 8000 vehicles running around London, excluding – excluding the 8300 buses […] emitting their fumes around our city. And I want to use our bulk buying power to electrify or hybridise as much of the fleet as possible. […] I hope thereby to […] help stimulate production so that I never again have to buy an internal combustion engine. I want to go electric and I think this city should go electric too.

In these difficult economic times we need a city that is attractive, where the air is clean, where the parks are safe, where the streets are lined with trees, where public transport is enjoyable to travel upon, where life on the streets is as calm and stress-free as possible. It makes us more globally competitive because people want to come and live here and work here and that is why we in City Hall have already […] diverted money from publicity budgets to invest six million pounds in […] our priority parks programme. […] And that's why we are spending four million pounds on planting ten thousand trees across some of the most deprived areas of Inner London.

I am delighted that Rosie Boycott has joined me as Chairman of the London Food Board and has launched a fantastic innovative plan to create two thousand and twelve new food-growing spaces by 2012. And we are exploring ways of making much wider use of green roofs (see Part 3) – the roofs that make up sixteen per cent of London's surface area.'

Look around London – only one per cent of journeys are being made by bicycle. […] in Copenhagen it is twenty per cent. Amsterdam it's thirty. In Norwich it's something like thirty per cent. […] I want to help people to get on their bikes […] it is perfectly safe in my view. What we are going to do to make people who don't feel safe is to help them with the experience of cycling by inaugurating a wonderful new London cycle hire scheme so that by 2010 we will have between six and ten thousand wonderful new bits of London infrastructure that you will be able to cycle on. And all the evidence from Paris is that it does entice people who do feel nervous about cycling or haven't cycled since university or for a long time to get on to their bikes. And I think that will be a great thing for the city. And that is why we are also of course going to be introducing our cycle superhighways for the same reason, starting off with twelve of them for the same reason because there are too many people who feel a little bit timid and I want to […] have space where people know that they are expected to cycle and that they can't be bullied out of the way by […] motorists […] I intend to champion cycling, the cleanest, greenest and most beautiful method of transport for as long as I am Mayor.

[…] I think it's our duty as politicians and it's my duty as Mayor to protect our green spaces; to make our cities, to make this city, London, more pleasant and more liveable, not just because we want to restrict CO_2, not just because we want to save the Planet, but also because if we want London to remain the greatest city on Earth then it makes complete economic sense to do so.

Analysis of Johnson's speech by John Vidal, Samantha Heath and Tony Day

(i) A journalist's view: John Vidal, Environment Editor, *Guardian*

John Vidal believes that Johnson's Environment Agency speech was the occasion when he 'came out' publicly as someone who now appears to take the problem of climate change seriously – in contrast to his previous attitude when, as a journalist, he derided it. It seems that the leadership of his party, the Conservatives, considered it inconceivable that he, as the head of one of the world's great cities, could remain a climate change sceptic, so it persuaded him to change his mind – at least publicly. But Vidal doubts that Johnson is entirely convinced: a few days later he took a decision not to implement a measure that would have helped cut London's carbon emissions – he refused to extend the Congestion Charging Zone further to the west of the city centre.

Vidal's explanation is that Johnson is essentially a populist politician – and an extremely good one at that – simply tailoring his message to appeal to two different audiences. Johnson's speech may have been a little disingenuous, but to Vidal it seemed honest in that he admitted to having changed his mind. Vidal believes that he will 'grow into the job' and, like most people who have taken the time to study the evidence, will soon genuinely accept the gravity of the climate situation and the need to act.

(ii) An NGO's analysis: Samantha Heath, Chief Executive, London Sustainability Exchange

Samantha Heath compares Boris Johnson, who appears to operate on an emotional or affective level, with his predecessor, Ken Livingstone, who was more analytical and technical in his approach. As the leader of an NGO, in lobbying a politician like Johnson she would therefore concentrate less on details and more on the overall vision of a policy. She also suggests that it's worth looking at the presence, or absence, of key 'buzz words' in politicians' speeches, as they can reveal which advisers have had the greatest influencing in briefing. For example, Johnson's avoidance of the phrase 'waste as a resource' suggests he may wish to indicate a rejection of the policies of previous advisers, for whom this phrase had become a mantra, and substitute his own concept of the problem.

She believes that some of the apparently new ideas proposed by Johnson, such as paying householders more if they recycle more, are not in fact new, and that this shows he may not have had enough time to study the situation thoroughly. Johnson seems to have his own overall vision but may want to show his advisers that he is a 'new broom' who wants to do things differently.

Her advice to those who wish to study the utterances of politicians is to look in detail at the exact wording of speeches and try to discover what specific, concrete actions they are proposing.

She also notices that Johnson fails to talk about what happens to waste after it has been sent for recycling: we should, she believes, also be urging people to buy products that contain recycled materials.

(iii) An academic's view: Tony Day, Professor of Energy Engineering, London South Bank University.

As an energy expert, Tony Day notices that only 11 lines in Johnson's speech are devoted to combined heat and power, and renewable energy is mentioned only once – but there are 47 lines devoted to cycling. This indicates where the mayor's real priorities lie.

Cycling may be a good thing, but is the overall policy a balanced one? However, Johnson's statements on CHP, though brief, are interesting: he reiterates clearly and unambiguously the GLA's commitment to provide 25% of London's energy from such 'local sources' by 2025. (The video here briefly illustrates some details of a typical combined heat and power installation, at Pimlico, near Victoria in London). Having made such a commitment, Day believes that Johnson has an obligation to deliver CHP and decentralised energy – and that indeed he sees evidence that the GLA is making a big effort to do so:

> The teams are in place, the analysis has been done, and the costings are being worked up.

However, on the subject of waste, Day finds Johnson's stated aim of delivering two-thirds of London's domestic electricity from waste difficult to understand: the numbers, he says, don't seem to add up. When politicians make a commitment on the public record, Day believes they should be held to that commitment:

> That's democracy in action.[…]

> Look for the numbers in a headline speech like this and say: 'Are they realistic?', 'Are they achievable?', and 'What do you have to do to get to them?' 'What policies have to be put in place now to make that potential a reality?'

SAQ 2.5   Key things to look for in a politician's speech

Summarise, on the basis of the three experts' comments, what they believe are some of the key things to look out for in a politician's speech.

Summary of Section 4

In this section you have viewed Boris Johnson's Environment Agency speech, heard commentaries on it from three experts, and attempted to distil a few of the key points to look out for when listening to politicians' speeches.

The bigger picture: the C40 Large Cities Climate Leadership Group

5

London, in addition to playing a leading role in tackling climate change within the UK, has taken a lead in encouraging similar developments in other major world cities. In 2005 the GLA convened the first meeting of the 'C40', a forum of 40 of the world's largest cities concerned about climate change. At a subsequent meeting in New York in May 2007, the mayors of the C40 cities joined with the Clinton Climate Initiative, led by ex-US President Bill Clinton, to announce the creation of the global Energy Efficiency Building Retrofit Programme (Figure 2.12). This brings together four of the world's largest Energy Service Companies (ESCOs), five of the world's largest banks and, initially, 16 of the largest cities. It offers building owners an energy audit to quantify their current energy use and building emissions; recommendations on a full range of measures to reduce emissions; a comprehensive, discounted offer of goods and services guaranteed to deliver the identified reductions; and an optional financing element to pay for the works, paid back through the guaranteed energy savings.

Figure 2.12 Launch of the Global Energy Efficiency Building Retrofit Programme at the C40 meeting in New York, 2007. Left to right: Mayor Bloomberg of New York; ex-US President Bill Clinton; Ken Livingstone, then Mayor of London

In February 2008 it was announced that two major energy service companies had won the first contracts to implement energy- and carbon-saving measures in London's public buildings. In the words of the mayor's announcement:

> World leading energy service companies Dalkia and Honeywell have been selected to help cut energy use in Greater London Authority buildings by 25 per cent and the Mayor will now launch a procurement process to let every public sector organization in London benefit from the same deal.
>
> London is the first city in the world to have completed the municipal tender process and appointed a company, following a deal developed by the Clinton Climate Initiative for the C40 group of cities [...]. The Mayor will also be working with the Clinton Climate Initiative to sign up private sector businesses to green their buildings.
>
> *(GLA, 2008)*

Boris Johnson, on succeeding Ken Livingstone as mayor, expressed his support for the C40 initiative. As he put it, in a press announcement to the C40 cities in June 2008:

> I am delighted to be working with the Mayor of Toronto and the C40 cities in recognition of my commitment for London to play a significant role in reducing carbon emissions and tackling climate change. London is a world leader in this area, and I am determined to see that the expertise and innovation being developed here is shared with cities around the world. Equally, I see many excellent ideas coming from other cities that we want to learn much more about – I have already committed to introduce a public bike hire scheme in London similar to that developed in Paris, another C40 city. Cities across the world share the common threat of climate change, and cities create most of the carbon emissions that are causing it, so it is vital we continue to work together to accelerate action on this issue.
>
> *(C40cities, 2008)*

Perhaps the highest-profile project resulting from the C40 and Clinton Climate Initiative's Building Retrofit Programme is the energy-efficient retrofitting of New York's most iconic landmark, the Empire State Building (Figure 2.13), described in Box 2.5.

Box 2.5   An energy-efficient retrofit for New York's Empire State Building

Figure 2.13 The Empire State Building in New York, a recent example of energy-efficient refurbishment of an iconic building

The Empire State Building is once again leading the way in the commercial building sector as it prepares to undergo an energy efficiency building retrofit project to improve building efficiency, reduce its carbon footprint, and save on utility costs. The Building Retrofit Program of the Clinton Climate Initiative (CCI) – designed to bring together many of the world's largest building owners, energy service companies, financial institutions, and cities to lower greenhouse gas emissions and energy consumption in existing buildings – is one of the key facilitators of the Empire State Building retrofit project. A cornerstone of the fight against climate change is to address emissions in existing buildings.

In the United States alone, existing buildings contribute 50 to almost 80 percent of urban greenhouse gas emissions. In addition, 80 percent of building lifecycle costs are incurred after initial construction, with 18 percent of this from utility costs alone [...].

As of March 2009, CCI has helped initiate more than 250 retrofit projects across the public and private sectors, encompassing over 500 million square feet of building space in more than 30 cities around the world.

From its inception, the retrofit of the Empire State Building has been a truly collaborative process. Under the leadership of owners

*LEED stands for Leadership in Energy and Environmental Design, the US 'Green Building' standard.

Empire State Building Company, a team comprised of Jones Lang LaSalle, Johnson Controls Inc., the Rocky Mountain Institute and CCI have worked to combine expertise and ingenuity to create a deeply sustainable project that sets a bar for building retrofit in the commercial building sector.

The Empire State Building will apply for LEED* certification under the U.S. Green Building Council's (USGBC) LEED program. With the increase in energy efficiency achieved by the project, and other sustainability measures undertaken by ESB ownership, the building will be able to pursue Gold level LEED certification as an existing building. The USGBC and CCI are strategic partners and are working together to accelerate the number of existing buildings that can achieve LEED certification, become more energy efficient and reduce their greenhouse gas emissions.

'One of the more remarkable takeaways from this historic retrofit project goes beyond the technical expertise and creativity – and that is the extraordinary benefit that comes from collaboration and teamwork,' said Kathy Baczko, CCI New York City Director. 'Although in some ways they could be considered competitors, all members of the Empire State Building team came together as partners right from the start. It was an honor for CCI to act as a convener and catalyst and then watch the experts deliver such amazing results. Our expectations are that the Empire State Building will show others the way by sharing these best practices.'

For many building owners, capital costs are a barrier to investing in building retrofits. Using energy performance contracting (EPC), a building retrofit generates guaranteed energy savings that, over a number of years, can be equal to the cost of the project including financing costs. Typically, owners can keep these savings or apply them toward the debt repayment on the project.

Using this EPC model, ownership can pursue maximum energy savings while minimizing the financial risks. Johnson Controls is providing a unique set of contracting terms and conditions including streamlined procurement, transparency in pricing, and other processes to reduce project cost and development time, and guarantees that the energy savings will be achieved.

The work includes several types of energy efficiency technologies including high-efficiency window glass replacement, redesigned heating and cooling systems and controls, lighting improvements, and radiative barriers. The project also incorporates behavior changes including management and operations updates and tenant engagement. Together these steps cost-effectively could reduce energy use by 38 percent and save 105,000 metric tons of greenhouse gas emissions over the next 15 years.

For CCI, this project also represents an exciting opportunity to work with a leading commercial building owner on a project using contract documents and tools created specifically for the commercial market by BOMA International and CCI.

The Empire State Building retrofit project will demonstrate that buildings can effectively reduce energy use and greenhouse gas emissions. It will show that a holistic building retrofit is a smart business proposition, which improves the building's marketability, asset value, and operating costs. For building owners and tenants – and the climate – commercial building retrofits can deliver a win-win outcome for all.

(esbsustainability, 2009)

The energy-efficient renovation of the Empire State Building is part of New York's 'PlaNYC 2030' announced by Mayor Bloomberg in 2007. PlaNYC aims to be a model for the twenty-first century. It focuses on five key areas: land, air, water, energy and transport, and includes the aim of reducing greenhouse gas emission by 30%.

The wider C40 grouping believes that in many cases cities are better placed than national governments to implement CO_2 reduction measures, so it urges national governments to:

- *Engage* more closely with their city leaders, whose responsibility for critical services mean they are best placed to deliver GHG [greenhouse gas] emissions reductions.

- *Empower* their city leaders so that where necessary they have the authority required to take action within cities to drive down GHG emissions.

- *Resource* their cities so that they are equipped with the relevant tools, services and finance to help deliver national targets.

(C40cities, 2009)

SAQ 2.6 CO_2 reduction actions

Now that you have studied London's climate change problems and potential solutions a bit more deeply, make a more detailed list of the CO_2 reduction actions that you consider most appropriate to (a) individuals (b) companies and organisations and (c) local, national and international governments.

Summary of Part 2

Having studied this part of the block, you will, I hope, have come to some conclusions of your own regarding the GLA's climate change strategy and initiatives. My tentative conclusion is that reducing global carbon emissions in cities and in the world as a whole will involve actions at all levels and comprising both behavioural and technological changes, in varying mixes depending on the context:

- by individual citizens, acting to reduce emissions in their households, workplaces, transport choices and local communities
- by citizens involving themselves in higher-level decisions about climate change by participating in the democratic process at local, city, national and international (EU) levels
- by companies and organisations, at small, medium and large scale, acting locally, nationally and internationally to embrace a 'low-carbon culture'
- by governments, acting to implement legislation and other measures to encourage carbon reduction at local, regional/city, national and international scales
- by governments setting an example through implementing low-carbon practices in their own buildings, travel and purchasing policies.

The material covered in this section supports the view that major cities like London are often better placed than national governments to undertake many of the key actions. They can also often move more quickly, so giving a lead to governments at national and international level – and at smaller-scale local government levels.

After completing Part 2 you should:

- understand how plans for cities to reduce carbon emissions may help to mitigate climate change
- appreciate that reductions in emissions are brought about by changes in people's behaviour as well as by technological 'fixes'
- recognise that major world cities can take a leading role and encourage others to tackle the climate change problem
- appreciate the different levels of responsibility (the individual, the market, society and the state) required to tackle climate change
- be aware that there are a variety of different approaches to problems and solutions, with varying degrees of success.

Answers to SAQs

SAQ 2.1

My list includes:

- promoting decentralised energy in London by requiring developers of new buildings to design energy-efficient buildings and to install combined heat and power plants and renewable energy systems (action by companies/ organisations, and by local government)

- encouraging the deployment of wind turbines and solar panels within London (action by organisations and individuals)

- installing solar panels at City Hall and Palestra, the headquarters of the London Development Agency (action by 'local' city government)

- funding a project to demonstrate low-emission hydrogen-fuelled buses in London and researching the potential for the hydrogen fuel to be derived from London's waste (action by 'local' city government – though the hydrogen buses project is part funded by the European Union, and therefore involves an element of international governmental action).

SAQ 2.2

Differences: the wedges in Figure 2.7 represent CO_2 savings that are much smaller than the 1 billion tonnes of CO_2 envisaged by Pacala and Socolow.

Pros: wedges break the problems of carbon emission reduction down into smaller and more manageable 'chunks'.

Cons: wedges can give the impression that dealing with climate change is relatively straightforward, but in practice it usually involves messy political conflicts and compromises. In addition, the wedges may give the impression that each measure is separate, whereas most of them are interdependent.

SAQ 2.3

(a) Bicycle hire scheme

This involves mainly behavioural change. Persuading Londoners in large numbers to abandon cars, buses and the 'tube' and take to bicycling is a significant behaviour-changing challenge, in view of the obstacles involved: perceived safety problems; adverse weather; security of cycles when parked, etc. That these problems can be largely overcome is shown by the very high levels of cycle use in many other developed European countries such as the Netherlands (admittedly flatter than London).

Cycling does of course involve technology but this is relatively simple, long established and well understood – although some of the detailed technological aspects of a bicycle hire scheme, probably involving the use of 'smart cards', locks, etc. are relatively new. The mayor also proposes to create dedicated 'bicycle motorways' which again involve little or no new technology but do involve significant planning and traffic management challenges.

(b) Electric vehicles

Here the challenges are mainly technological. Current electric vehicles (EVs) have relatively low carbon emissions (depending on the source of the electricity that powers them), but have limited range compared with conventional fossil-fuelled vehicles. However, this limitation seems likely to be overcome by improved batteries in the medium-term future. The widespread use of EVs does involve the installation of many thousands of charging points in homes, workplaces, shops, car parks, etc. If the technological problems can be overcome, as seems probable, then the everyday use of EVs should involve only relatively modest behavioural changes.

(c) A transport carbon reduction measure that is all behavioural and does not involve technology is, of course, a shift towards walking as a mode of travel. A significant proportion of Londoners could probably be encouraged to travel on foot if there were more and better footpaths and improved signage – plus additional measures to reduce the risk of being run over by drivers of cars, vans and lorries.

SAQ 2.4

In Part 1, Figure 1.36 the stages were identified as:

1   recognition of a problem and its scale

2   gathering relevant data

3   getting backing – from scientists, the press, the public and politicians

4   planning and costing appropriate solutions

5   implementing the solutions

6   living with the consequences.

In tackling the climate change problem in London, Stage 1 was reached when leading politicians like Ken Livingstone (before he was elected mayor) recognised the problem in the 1990s (led in turn by reports such as those of the Intergovernmental Panel on Climate Change).

Stage 2 was reached when the Greater London Authority started gathering data on London's greenhouse gas emissions.

Stage 3 was reached with the publication from 2004 of a succession of reports analysing the problem and proposing solutions. There was also an increased recognition that cities, as very large fossil fuel consumers, should play a major role in climate change mitigation.

Stages 4 and 5 involved setting up the London Climate Change Agency.

Stage 6 involved the re-election of Ken Livingstone in 2004 and the continuation of the climate change policies and actions he had initiated during his first term of office; it also involves Livingstone's replacement in 2008 by Boris Johnson with a somewhat different set of political priorities and actions.

SAQ 2.5

My list included the following points:

- Why are they saying it?
- What is the main audience to which their words are addressed (not necessarily just the audience in the room)?
- Look out for 'buzz words'.
- Is the politician's style principally an intellectual one, or does he/she mainly operate at an emotional or 'affective' level?
- Look for the numbers: are they realistic?
- What concrete actions are being proposed and are they achievable?

SAQ 2.6

(a) Individuals

Installing insulation, draught-stripping, efficient heating, lighting and appliances, plus solar water heating and photovoltaics. Travelling less and switching to low-carbon travel modes; driving economically with lower consumption cars/vans. Lowering house temperatures and lighting levels, etc.

(b) Companies and organisations

As above plus installing combined heat and power plant and renewable energy technologies, e.g. wind turbines or solar arrays, in suitable locations.

(c) Local, national and international governments

Creating regulations and incentives to encourage individuals, companies and organisations to install low-carbon systems for heating, electricity and transport. Government can also do many of these things itself, for its own buildings, vehicles, etc., and for the wider community as a whole.

References

Boyle, G., Everett, B. and Ramage, J. (eds) (2003) *Energy Systems and Sustainability, Power for a Sustainable Future*, Oxford, Oxford University Press/Milton Keynes, The Open University.

Committee on Climate Change (2008) *Building a Low Carbon Economy: the UK's Contribution to Tackling Climate Change*, London, The Stationery Office.

C40cities (2008) 'Mayor of Toronto to chair C40 group to continue climate change co-operation across world's cities', Climate Leadership Group News Release, 4 June, http://www.c40cities.org/about/goals.jsp (Accessed 7 October 2009).

C40cities (2009) 'C40 goals for UNFCCC: Poznan to Copenhagen: Engage Empower Resource', Climate Leadership Group, http://www.c40cities.org/news/news-20080604.jsp (Accessed 7 October 2009).

Day, A. R., Ogumka, P., Jones, P. G. and Dunsdon, A. (2009) 'The use of the planning system to encourage low carbon energy technologies in buildings', *Renewable Energy* vol. 34, pp. 2016–21.

DECC (2009a) *The UK Low Carbon Transition Plan: National Strategy for Climate and Energy*, Department of Energy and Climate Change, July.

DECC (2009b) *The UK Renewable Energy Strategy*, Department of Energy and Climate Change, July.

DEFRA (2008) *Environment in Your Pocket 2008*, Department of Environment, Food and Rural Affairs.

esbsustainability (2009) 'Cities and climate change, Empire State Building', 6 April, http://esbsustainability.com/SocMe/?id=246&pid=237&sid=246&Title=Cities%2C+buildings%2C+and+climate+change&Template=Project (Accessed 7 October 2009).

Everett, B. (2003) 'Electricity', in Boyle et al. (eds) (2003).

Gavron, N. (2007) 'Deputy Mayor's Foreword', in GLA (2007), *Action Today to Protect Tomorrow: The Mayor's Climate Change Action Plan*, Greater London Authority, pp. vii–viii.

GLA (2004) *Green Light to Clean Power: The Mayor's Energy Strategy*, Greater London Authority.

GLA (2007) *Action Today to Protect Tomorrow: The Mayor's Climate Change Action Plan*, Greater London Authority.

GLA (2008) 'Mayor announces start of a groundbreaking programme to green London's public buildings', Press Release, Greater London Authority, 28 February, http://mayor.london.gov.uk/view_press_release.jsp?releaseid=16634 (Accessed 13 October 2009).

GLA (2009) *An Electric Vehicle Delivery Plan for London*, Greater London Authority.

Intergovernmental Panel on Climate Change (2001) *Third Assessment Report*, IPCC.

Intergovernmental Panel on Climate Change (2007) *Fourth Assessment Report: Summary for Policy Makers*, IPCC.

Livingstone, K. (2007) Mayor's Foreword in GLA, (2007), *Action Today to Protect Tomorrow: The Mayor's Climate Change Action Plan*, Greater London Authority, pp. iii–vi.

London Assembly (2009) *Report by the Budget and Performance Committee on the GLA Group Environment Spend 2009/10*, Greater London Authority.

London First (2008) *Cutting the Capital's Carbon Footprint: Delivering Decentralised Energy*, London First, October.

Science (2008) 'Reimagining Cities', Special Issue, 8 February, various articles.

Starke, L. (ed) (2007) *State of the World: Our Urban Future*, Worldwatch Institute Report, New York and London, W.W. Norton.

Stern, N. (2006) *The Economics of Climate Change*, Cabinet office – HM Treasury, Cambridge, Cambridge University Press.

United Nations (2007) *World Urbanisation Prospects: the 2007 Revision*, Population Database, New York, United Nations, http://esa.un.org/unup/ (Accessed June 2008).

Wikipedia (2009) 'London', http://en.wikipedia.org/wiki/London#cite_note-politics_uk-9 (Accessed 7 October 2009).

Part 3
Facing the future

Roger Blackmore

Introduction

1

In Parts 1 and 2 you explored how people living in cities, the main drivers of global environmental change, confronted past environmental problems and are now striving to reduce their environmental impact. Part 1 discussed how London responded to two major pollution challenges in the past and how it had to adapt to survive. Part 2 discussed how the leaders of modern London, together with those of other cities, are trying to avoid contributing to future problems from climate change by taking steps to reduce its carbon footprint.

How cities and their populations respond to the environmental challenges of the future is one of the key issues of the twenty-first century, because as Girardet explains in *Creating Sustainable Cities*:

> The cities we build and the urban lifestyles we lead today will profoundly affect the chances of coming generations to shape their *own* future.

> *(Girardet, 1999, p. 13)*

He calculates that cities and towns now use three-quarters of the world's resources and produce three-quarters of the world's waste. But he also makes the point that cities are 'structures that are fossilised upon a landscape' and can be expected to last for a very long time. The decisions we make today in planning and designing buildings and cities will influence the opportunities and lifestyles of generations to come and should take into account these long-term needs. He argues that there are many ways of dramatically improving the environmental performance of cities, reducing energy consumption and resource use and waste, for example, in ways that will also improve urban living in cities through imaginative approaches to transport and use of urban spaces. While this requires sustainable policies and appropriate use of new technology, as described in Parts 1 and 2, he also argues for a new *culture* of sustainability:

> Can we make *civilisation* come back to life again in cities? Can we put the pulsing heart of conviviality back into our cities? How can we make sure of creating *cities of diversity* for the new millennium – places of cultural vigour, of lively encounters and physical beauty that are also sustainable in economic and environmental terms?

> […] The tools, techniques and partnerships that can help us achieve environmental and social sustainability and human well-being in the age of the city will also be central to creating a sustainable relationship between people and planet. In addition, we need to remind ourselves that cities aren't only places for humans, but that city people co-exist with trees, plants and animals that need their own distinct urban habitats.

> *(Girardet, 1999, p. 12)*

Part 3 takes up this challenge by asking you to imagine what new shapes and directions the cities of the future might take, first by looking at the early development of modern transport in London, then at plans for two completely new eco-cities. It then explores examples of 'greening' our existing cities. It moves on to look at how cities now have to adapt to environmental change, to cope with threats such as heatwaves and floods to which cities are particularly vulnerable. Cities have always shown enormous capacity to adapt and survive, but the question now is *how* to adapt in smart ways that can help to reduce the impacts of environmental change, in other words to work more with nature than against it. Part of that approach means learning to value urban biodiversity and to understand how it is adapting to new environments in our cities.

Part 3 ends by applying ideas and techniques that you have learnt during the course to assess action to improve environmental performance both at the global and city level, and also for communities and individuals seeking to 'make a difference'.

Re-imagining the city

2

This section explores some positive initiatives that can be taken to develop more sustainable cities – cities that are both good to live in and have a much reduced environmental impact – and suggests some ecological principles that need to be followed. It compares and contrasts two approaches to improving cities: building eco-cities and greening cities. But first, it looks at how different transport systems evolved in London to help understand how the modern city developed.

As argued in Part 1, Section 2, the transport of people and goods has always been vital to major cities, but managing these flows and their impacts can be difficult. Take the car, for example. As a first step to re-imagining the city, try to think of a city without cars. Cars in the UK still account for over 90% of all journeys, and road networks designed for cars, vans and lorries dominate the landscape of cities, countryside and suburbs. In the second half of the twentieth century, cities were designed for the movement of cars rather than pedestrians or cyclists who, if they were lucky, were confined to narrow strips of pavement or the edge of the road, while public transport was also marginalised. In recent years, however, problems with congestion and pollution and a growing awareness of the economic and environmental costs of fossil fuels have raised questions about the dominant role of road vehicles. Some authorities have started to modify their city centre streets to create pedestrian areas, while other city or regional authorities attempt to control access of road vehicles to the most congested areas. Almost all these initiatives, however, are controversial when proposed and today it is still hard to imagine a city, town or village in the UK without cars.

The road network across the country as well as within cities, towns and villages is an example of Girardet's 'structures that are fossilised upon a landscape'. It is an infrastructure that has taken decades to build and will continue to influence the shape of new developments for decades to come. This is in part because it would be expensive and disruptive to design a new network from scratch, but in part because we find it difficult to imagine replacing our cars and vans, even though the disadvantages of this form of transport may be mounting. One figure for me captures the contradictions of managing urban road transport today. In 2009, traffic in Central London moved at an average of 15 kph, no faster than it did over a hundred years ago in 1900, when vehicles were pulled by horses.

Before looking at what the cities of the future might look like we will turn, one last time, to London's past, to the age of horse-drawn vehicles, to find out what a city without cars was like and explore the choices our ancestors made in moving to mechanised transport. The results may surprise you – they certainly surprised me when I first found out about them – and may help to show that alternatives to petrol or diesel vehicles have always been available. What pressures influenced the inhabitants of many European towns and cities to consider alternatives to horse power? Part of the reason is that any technology that performs a useful service also has its downsides, even one as simple as horse-drawn transport. The economic and environmental disadvantages of using horse power in a large city were becoming very apparent, as this passage on London explains:

> [In] 1900 virtually every vehicle on the streets of London was horse-drawn. More than 300,000 horses were needed to keep the city on the move, hauling everything from private carriages and cabs to buses, trams and delivery vans [...]
>
> Fifty-thousand horses [alone] were required to keep Victorian London's public transport running. According to one writer of the time, these horses ate their way through a quarter of a million acres of foodstuff per year, and deposited 1000 tonnes of dung on the roads every day. The disposal of large quantities of horse droppings was a major problem. Dung could make the roads hazardous and unpleasant when wet. Crossing sweepers made meagre earnings clearing a path for pedestrians to cross roads and dung carts collected and deposited droppings on vast dung heaps in the poorer parts of town each day.
>
> To keep a single bus or tram on the road for 12 hours each day a team of 12 horses was required, each one harnessed for 3 to 4 hours and travelling about 15 miles. The horses needed to be fed, watered, stabled and groomed, and tended by blacksmiths and vets. Caring for the horses represented up to 55% of operating costs and was even greater if feed prices rose (such as following a poor harvest). The LGOC [London General Omnibus Company] spent about £20 000 each year on horseshoes alone.
>
> *(London Transport Museum, 2007 and 2008)*

Problems such as these encouraged public operators to look for cheaper and more efficient ways of transporting people and goods. Within the next 20 years, transport in London (and many other European cities) was transformed; buses and trams no longer used horse power but new, cleaner forms of motive power. The most popular form of passenger transport in London (and probably many other towns in the UK) became the tram, which was powered by electric motors taking electricity from the track network. During this time more Londoners were travelling by tram than by any other form of transport. By the end of the 1920s, London had the largest tram network in the country, with 345 miles of track being served by 2600 electric tramcars (Figure 3.1). While Londoners travelled on electric trams overground, they also had access to what was then the most advanced rapid transit system in the world, the London Underground, a network of underground railways whose locomotives were also powered by electricity. In other words, about a hundred years ago London's transport was largely car free and running on quiet, clean electricity (though coal power stations were used to generate the electricity), a situation that many cities around the world are trying to recreate today (though with cleaner energy sources).

(a)

(b)

(c)

Figure 3.1 The evolution of trams in the UK: (a) horse-drawn tram in Stamford Hill, London; (b) London electric tram in the 1920s; (c) modern tram in Sheffield

But it didn't last. This new form of transport was a great improvement on horsepower: it was cleaner, more reliable and provided greater capacity, giving Londoners more mobility. But it also had several disadvantages that led trams to come under pressure from alternatives. The rail tracks were expensive to maintain and caused disruption when they were laid down or replaced and made journeys uncomfortable. Buses proved cheaper to run, and with pneumatic tyres were more comfortable for passengers, and more flexible to use. In the 1930s both petrol-driven buses and electric trolleybuses (powered by overhead lines) began to replace the tram, which disappeared completely in 1952. In the last decade, however, the tram has begun to make a comeback in the form of a new light rail transit system in south London (and of course many other UK towns), following the lead of many continental European cities.

One major downside that has accompanied the rise of all forms of mechanised road transport, but particularly the motor car, has been death and injury from traffic accidents. It has long been one of the major causes of death and injury, first in Europe and North America, and more recently globally, particularly for children, yet curiously it seems to be accepted as part of the price we accept for the freedom to travel. Even though cars were rare in the UK in the 1920s and 1930s, many early drivers were lethal. Deaths from road traffic accidents in London increased nearly tenfold to more than 1300 by 1929 – and trams were not the major cause – so that driving tests and a 30 mph urban speed limit were introduced in 1934.

What can this short account of the rise and fall of the electric tram, with its focus on trams and buses, tell us about cities and their transport systems? First, it demonstrates that there have been successful road transport systems that used an electricity grid as their main power source, in preference to the petrol or diesel engine. Admittedly, this was in large part due to the lack of serious competition from the early internal combustion engines and private motor cars. Second, this new transport system and the network of tracks that it built lasted for several decades. Third, although it solved many of the problems arising from horse-drawn transport, it still had shortcomings. Other forms of transport appeared to offer better solutions to these problems.

SAQ 3.1   Changing patterns of public transport

1   What economic and environmental reasons have been given for the changes in public transport in London at the beginning of the twentieth century, first from horse-drawn vehicles to electric trams, then from electric trams to buses?

2   How were the lives of Londoners affected by these changes?

It seems likely that the main motivations behind the changes of transport described here were economic and social, although the environmental nuisance from horse manure may have provided a strong incentive to act decisively and quickly (see the 'Great Stink' discussed in Part 1). During the first half of the twentieth century the collaboration between wealthy city councils and private enterprise led to a drive towards modernisation. They were eager to adopt the latest technology and to seek out cost savings. The flexibility of buses, the freedom offered by the car and, from the 1950s onwards, the falling cost of buying and fuelling private vehicles led to the age of the car, and to city centres being designed to accommodate them. Although town planning kept an eye on land use, including the idea of 'green belts' surrounding large towns, it did not stop satellite towns and suburbs serviced by cars and buses spreading out across much of the country. The idea of cheap fuel for heating or for private transport was seen to be of obvious benefit to everyone, summed up by the proud boast of the new nuclear industry that electricity would soon be 'too cheap to meter'. This optimism for the future of the car was illustrated in the design of the new town of Milton Keynes with its grid-like network of roads and multiple centres – and it is now the fastest-growing city in the country.

This approach to town development is based on a view that cities serve economic and social needs, but also the assumption that the Earth's resources can be extracted and disposed of cheaply by ever better techniques. Industrialisation and ingenuity have given us access to more resources than ever before and have brought great benefits. If energy, materials and land are cheap, why shouldn't everyone live the 'American dream' of a large house packed with appliances and several cars in the drive? The availability of cheap and limitless material goods and energy has led to wasteful habits not just in individuals, but in the way cities have developed to serve and encourage consumption rather than the careful use of resources – if something is cheap and plentiful, why bother to use it carefully? Unfortunately, the assumption that a growing global population can continue to have access to endless, cheap resources is no longer tenable; this way of living cannot be sustained for much longer. Girardet provides a working definition for a sustainable city that emphasises the long-term needs of people:

> A sustainable city is organised so as to enable all its citizens to meet their own needs and to enhance their well-being without damaging the natural world or endangering the living conditions of other people, now or in the future.

> *(Girardet, 1999, p. 13)*

But what principles should guide the design and organisation of more sustainable cities? Academics and pressure groups have argued for several decades that the modern city needs to be redesigned in order to function better, and should incorporate ecological principles that have largely been ignored until recently. In particular, as you saw in Part 2, there have been growing movements to steer cities to become more careful in their use of energy and materials. Most of these have been concerned with making steady improvements in making cities 'greener', for example tightening regulations to improve the insulation of buildings, and introducing recycling schemes for residents and businesses – essentially modifying and improving the existing housing stocks and urban infrastructures. Some, the proponents of eco-cities, say that we have to be much more radical in our attitude to cities; that they need to be redesigned completely to avoid global environmental disaster.

Whether the approach is to modify the existing components of a city or to design a new city from scratch, the ecological principles they are based on are similar. We can learn from natural ecosystems where organisms compete for the basics of life: energy, water and nutrients. Little is wasted and the resources are endlessly reused or recycled as one organism's waste becomes another's food. Cities can also be thought of in terms of what they consume and throw out. When examined in this light the inefficiency and waste of many modern cities becomes more obvious, as Girardet explains:

> Nature's own ecosystems have an essentially *circular* metabolism in which every output which is discharged by an organism also becomes an input which renews and sustains the continuity of the whole living environment of which it is a part. The whole web of life hangs together in a 'chain of mutual benefit', through the flow of nutrients that pass from one organism to another.
>
> The metabolism of most modern cities, in contrast, is essentially *linear*, with resources being 'pumped' through the urban system without much concern about their origin or about the destination of wastes, resulting in the discharge of vast amounts of waste products incompatible with natural systems. In urban management, inputs and outputs are considered as largely unconnected. Food is imported into cities, consumed, and discharged as sewage into rivers and coastal waters. Raw materials are extracted from nature, combined and processed into consumer goods that ultimately end up as rubbish which can't be beneficially reabsorbed into the natural world.

(*Girardet, 1999, pp. 32, 33*)

The challenge, whether looking at part of a city or the whole, is to redesign cities to function more like ecosystems – to use as few external resources as possible other than those which can be sustainably renewed – while maintaining a quality of life that we would all wish for. This is what I mean by re-imagining cities.

How would a sustainable city designed on ecological principles, an ***eco-city***, be realised in practice? One of the leading exponents of eco-cities is Richard Register, an American artist who was the first to use the term 'eco-city' to describe a sustainable city that provides almost all of its own food and energy, and minimises pollution by reusing or recycling most of its waste (Register, 1987). Read through the following excerpts from a recent interview with Richard Register and make a note of the design features or structures he thinks are important to achieve these aims, then answer the questions at the end:

David Room

What are ecological cities?

Richard Register

Ecological cities are cities that are ecologically healthy and we don't really have any yet, so that's a very big challenge to design and actually build them. An ecologically healthy city would be one that gets along with all the other plants and animals on the planet, that supports people and their compassionate creative activities in their lives and is healthy in the long term for evolution itself. I think that's the bottom line for cities: if they can get along with the planet they live on, then they're ecological cities.

David Room

What are some leading examples of ecological city design?

Richard Register

Well, there are many examples of pieces of ecological design that you find in cities all over the world. You find some of the larger pieces in the sense of the layout of the city in Curitiba, Brazil for example, Portland, Oregon and some other cities where there is a very strong connection between the transit system and the structure of the city. The idea usually is to make the city more three-dimensional, like living systems are normally three-dimensional and not flat; complex living systems don't take the form of a sheet of paper. Similarly if you spread out cities and make them very flat, like modern suburbs [they] are extraordinarily inefficient and don't work. So a lot of ecological city design is working with density and diversity in close proximity, and if you can accomplish that you're well on your way. In Curitiba, Brazil, for example, there are five long arms that reach out from a pedestrian centre. Along those arms there is high-density development and a dedicated bus line, meaning it is for buses only, and not for automobiles. And so in a context like that you can have very rapid transit for lots of people who actually live along the transit. And then in Curitiba, Brazil they have very low density or no density at all, in other words natural areas, river restorations [and] so on beyond the arms of high-density development. So it's an articulation there of living, working, transit all being held together in a fairly small area. And the result is they save lots of energy, they don't produce a lot of pollution and they have plenty of room for many of the other aspects of an ecologically healthy city, one of them being very efficient recycling, restoration of natural areas, bicycle and pedestrian paths and a lot of other things. So that's a beginning. Other examples from history include places like Venice, Italy, the city that's held together by bridges and waterways and no cars at all. Like that you can begin to explore the whole concept from little pieces and overall general pattern.

David Room

What has been the historical pattern of city design?

Richard Register

Well, an interesting thing historically speaking is that most cities before the automobile came around were based very largely on pedestrian access and had this logic of access by proximity, as I call it, in their bones you might say. In other words they were designed so that people could walk most places to get what they needed. And so that was the historic pattern until trains came along and cities began moving out to points farther away from the centre. Streetcars and so on, and then with sprawl, the city blew out all over the landscape and so were very difficult to hold together after that.

[…]

David Room

How does energy consumption relate to city structure?

Richard Register

Well, basically the flatter the city, the more dependent on cars of course, the more energy consumption you're going to have. And not only cars of course but remember trucks are involved in this as well. And so virtually everything once you establish a flat city becomes very energy consuming just to hold the activities of the city together. So the structure of the city has everything to do with the amount of energy that is required. Probably the lowest-energy city would have the highest diversity and be the most compact and you can imagine holding the whole thing together by foot power and elevators and maybe recourse to some people movers, you know the conveyor belts you have at airports. So that would be the super most dense pedestrian orientated city and probably would be the least energy consuming and certainly the most conserving in terms of land. So the compact city goes a long way towards solving a lot of those problems, without even putting any effort into it other than just the logic of the proximity making some kind of sense. New York runs on about half the average per capita energy use of cities around the United States. It's very compact. People get around by transit there and there's a lot of mixed use close together. So those are dynamics you can work with. Now they've been neglected and where energy has gone into thinking through the built infrastructure, mostly it's around buildings and making buildings more energy efficient with insulation, maybe building solar greenhouses, natural day lighting and some places in the world such as in Germany there's a lot of interest in rooftop gardening and greening of the roofs. So all these things count for a lot. But to actually look at the basic structure of the city is the Holy Grail if you're going to have a healthy civilization in the future, how you're actually going to build that civilization, it will come down to solving the problem of how to build the cities. And of course that's very deeply involved in the amount of energy that flows through. I maintain that if we are to build ecologically healthy cities we could run the whole civilization on maybe ten percent of the energy that we use now.

(Global Public Media, 2004)

SAQ 3.2   How to design an eco-city

1   What structures should eco-cities use, according to Register?

2   What features of early towns or cities could be used in eco-cities and why?

According to Register, there is now no alternative but to start building eco-cities (Figure 3.2), and radically redesign villages, towns and cities. If his claim is correct, that a world with 'ecologically healthy cities' would use only one-tenth of the energy now used, it is worth serious consideration. He is dismissive, however, of what he calls 'half-way eco-cities' that still rely on cars and high energy use, even if both are used efficiently and recycling is thorough. Not everyone would agree with such a radical approach. Some are also critical of the eco-city movement and say that eco-cities are neither practical nor even desirable. They would point out that there are few if any existing cities or towns that meet these strict criteria. Others who are in favour of the concept would argue that it is far more effective at the moment to concentrate efforts on reducing the impacts of existing urban areas, where over half of the world already lives. This means developing new standards and designs in stages, if as quickly as possible, rather than trying to create a perfect design for a very few people.

The next section describes two eco-cities that are intended to be built in the near future and the principles behind them. You can check for yourself how far they follow the ecological principles described by Girardet and Register and use your understanding of sustainability to assess their viability.

Figure 3.2 Designs for eco-cities: (a) Hamburg harbour, Germany; (b) floating cities – 'Lilypads' for climate change refugees; (c); Tianjin, China; (d) 'plastic cell' dwellings; (e) paper log houses (temporary housing built from paper tubes)

2.1 Welcome to the eco-city

This section is resource based, that is, it makes use of a set of resources – one complete article, some excerpts and pictures from another article, and a video from the course DVD. The resources describe the plans for building two eco-cities. The first is Dongtan, in China, planned to be built on Chongming Island in the delta of the Yangtze River close to the city of Shanghai. The second is Masdar, planned for a much smaller, but rich country, the United Arab Emirates, in the Middle East. The complete article (Pool, 2009) comes from a journal on environmental technology and, not surprisingly, explores the technical aspects in some detail. The excerpts from the second article come from the magazine *BBC Focus* (Taylor, 2008, p. 46), which is aimed at the general reader and uses diagrams and pictures as well as text to convey information. The video on the course DVD looks at Dongtan and compares the merits of building eco-cities with modifying existing cities.

These resources present a lot of information. Rather than trying to take in or memorise all the detail I suggest you read and view them with specific purposes in mind. To that end you will be asked to carry out three tasks to help you make sense of this information. However, before making a start, pause for a moment to think whether eco-cities can make a realistic contribution to a sustainable future.

Activity 3.1   Are eco-cities the answer to sustainable living?

What questions would you ask about the design and implementation of an eco-city if it is to meet the long-term needs of people? Assume that the eco-city will meet all the required environmental criteria and concentrate on the social and economic dimensions of sustainability discussed in Block 6 and the discussion 'What is a city?' at the beginning of the block.

Discussion

Social: One possible problem with eco-cities is that they are design solutions produced by individual experts or groups of experts. One question to ask is to what extent are the communities who are going to live in eco-cities involved in decisions, who decides who lives there, and how much say will they have in the planning and evolution of the eco-city? Also, how 'open' are the cities to adapting to changing circumstances, or changing demands from their inhabitants?

Economic: Building new cities from scratch, often using state-of-the-art technology, is likely to be very expensive and some may not function well or as intended. Such projects need rich sponsors or state subsidies, with the possibility of failure if this is withdrawn. The article by Pool points out that the future of Dongtan is now in doubt because of the loss of a key supporter.

Overall comment: Building model cities or towns is not a new idea, nor is the idea of making them more ecological, but designing whole towns from scratch and arranging for communities to live in them as eco-cities is a new venture. There are no well-tested rules to follow to guarantee success and mark a change from the more usual mix of planned and unplanned growth of cities. These are experimental prototypes for new cities, not a mass model. Eco-cities are in the experimental phase and are sometimes described as laboratories for future living. Remember these points as you read through the next section.

Your first task is to read the article ('A tale of two cities') and excerpt ('Welcome to Eco-city') to find out the extent to which the planning for these two real eco-cities follows the ecological principles outlined by Register and Girardet and discussed in SAQ 3.2, namely:

- use of compactness in the design of the cities
- use of diversity of building types and spaces
- catering for a range of different people
- efficiency in use of resources
- use of renewable resources
- reducing waste by recycling resources.

The second task is to compare and contrast some similarities and differences in how the two eco-cities achieve their aims, specifically:

- Who is involved in the planning?
- How are the two cities adapted to their local environment?

As you work through the article and excerpt make your own notes on these points, then answer SAQs 3.3 and 3.4.

A tale of two cities

Rebecca Pool

IET Knowledge Network, 20 April 2009

As oil-rich Abu Dhabi builds the 'world's greenest' city, carbon-heavy China has designs on an eco-friendly metropolis. *E&T* takes a look.

Exactly when the world decided eco-villages just weren't big enough is difficult to gauge, but for today's environmentally friendly developments, size is everything. Forget any ideals of holistic living and group-hugs; the present-day eco-city is big, bold, sophisticated and requires a lot of cash.

Roger Wood, an associate director of Arup, the global engineering consultancy that designed Chinese eco-city, Dongtan, is only too aware of this fact. In 2005, Dongtan was destined to be built on Chongming, at the mouth of China's Yangtze River. While the alluvial island had looked like the ideal site to build yet another sprawl of commuter towns, its city planners, backed by the Chinese government and funded by Shanghai Industrial Investment Corporation, decided to build an eco-city, ready for 5,000 residents by 2010, instead. However, spool forward to 2009 and the outlook is somewhat different.

First, government backing is now less certain, with media reports saying Dongtan's key political supporter is now under house arrest for fraud. Second, the worldwide recession means funds are no longer flowing. Put simply, the project has stalled with construction yet to start.

As Wood explains: 'The issue we have with all of this is over whether there is enough government policy. We were hoping to get all the permissions in place to build the first phase by 2010, but the permissions have dragged on and, given the current economic situation, we are not sure when this phase will be delivered.'

This is a pity as Dongtan not only makes a stunning template for future projects but, when built, will exhibit a myriad of innovative designs and technologies. The 30 km^2 site, eventually housing [500,000] residents, will consist of three villages linked to Shanghai by a new rail and road link.

Dongtan details

From the start, Wood says his designers wanted to reduce the amount of any resource used in the city, be it in construction or the daily use of electricity. As a result, the city will require 66 per cent less power than a conventional development, with energy coming from wind turbines, solar panels and biological sources such as human sewage and municipal waste. Indeed a combined heat and power plant is expected to burn waste rice husks.

'We want to produce energy from a reliable renewable source, so biomass is one solution,' adds Wood. 'We asked ourselves, where can we find a waste product that's already done what it's done so we're not adding to the carbon footprint by [growing] it. We came up with rice husks and sewage.'

Wood also looked to minimise energy use in transport, but rather than specifying Dongtan a car-free zone, he's decided the city will have zero-emissions transport, running on either electricity or hydrogen. Electricity will come from renewable sources while plans are in place to build a renewable energy plant to create the electricity needed to produce hydrogen.

When dealing with waste the designers hope to implement an automated vacuum collection system. Here, waste is transported at high speeds through underground tunnels to a building where it is collected.

'You put your waste in a bin and it gets sucked along to a particular place,' explains Wood. 'This means you only need one place where vehicles come to collect refuse from, instead of driving to every single house, and so saving energy.'

And, because Dongtan will be built on what is currently farm land, Wood felt the agriculture production of the city should equal that of the present land. Not easy, although factories that produce organic food under artificial light have been designed into the plans.

Clearly achieving 'zero-carbon' status is no mean feat, and, technology aside, Wood believes urban planning is crucial. 'You need to plan a city to encourage these things to work, and once you do this the situation will snowball,' asserts Wood. 'It has to be easy to walk, cycle or catch a bus to go to the shops or go to work, so you have to make the employment, facilities and housing all close together.'

Indeed, Dongtan is designed so every single resident will be no more than a seven-minute walk from public transport. And, while cars are allowed into the eco-city, its three villages are planned so this isn't necessary.

Wood also worked hard to design a city where people would actually want to work, rest and play. Looking carefully at optimum dwelling density, he decided that low-rise but high-density living would achieve this while still being economical.

'Shanghai has 250 to 300 dwellings per hectare packed into tall towers, but we felt this wouldn't work in Dongtan,' he says. 'So we are thinking of five-to eight-storey dwellings, with 75 per hectare. This is equivalent to say west Kensington in London.'

Buildings will be constructed predominantly with timber, with stringent criteria set out regarding the use of renewable or reclaimed sources. 'We hope there will [be] an element of pre-fabrication to minimise waste, but we don't want the dwellings to look like the same little box, we want freedom of design as well,' adds Wood.

Masdar City

The opposite holds true for Masdar City, where construction is in full swing some 17 km east of Abu Dhabi in the United Arab Emirates. Spearheaded by the Government of Abu Dhabi, the 'world's first zero-carbon, zero-waste city' will cost an incredible US$22bn, span 6.5 km^2, house 40,000 residents and support 1,500 businesses. A recently completed 10 MW solar plant – the largest of its kind in the Middle East – will power construction, which should come to an end by 2015.

The city's figures may impress, but its credentials deliver real clout. The project was designed by British architects Foster and Partners, famed for high-profile glass and steel buildings including the London Gherkin and Beijing Capital International Airport.

It has support from global conservation charity the World Wide Fund for Nature, while organisations around the world, including BP, Rolls-Royce and GE, are clamouring to get on board. Cooperation with the Massachusetts Institute of Technology has paved the way to the Masdar Institute of Science and Technology, which will open in September of this year, welcoming in 38 postgraduates and staff, the city's first residents.

As Norman Foster of Foster and Partners put it: 'The environmental ambitions of the Masdar Initiative are a world first … Masdar promises to set new benchmarks for the sustainable city of the future.'

So what exactly are these benchmarks? Once built, the city will consume only 20 per cent as much energy as a similar-sized conventional city and will be completely powered by solar energy. Roofs, canopies and land on the city's edge will support photovoltaics while a concentrating solar power plant will provide the city with the electricity it needs to keep cool under the blistering Abu Dhabi sun.

Keeping cool is crucial. In July and August, Abu Dhabi temperatures top 50 °C, so a first design step was to orient the city north east to south west. This helps to minimise the amount of direct sunlight on buildings while still providing enough natural sunlight.

According to Foster and Partners architect Gerard Evenden, building designs incorporate heavily insulated walls with thin layers of copper foil on the outside to keep heat out and hopefully prevent residents reaching for the air-conditioning. Evenden has also made Masdar City a car-free zone, so the entire development is being built with narrow, shaded passage-ways, instead of roads, which will funnel breezes and help to keep the city cool. Pillars will also raise the city off the ground, making space for a personal rapid transport network of compact, driverless 'podcars'.

Water conservation

Unlike heat, water is an increasingly sparse resource in and around Abu Dhabi and while Masdar City will have a solar-powered desalination plant, around 80 per cent of water will be recycled. Dew catchers, rainwater harvesting and electronic sensors to detect cracked pipes will all be used and dedicated green spaces will be planted with drought-resistant plants, not lawns. And as part of the zero-waste strategy, biological waste will be processed into fuel or used to create nutrient-rich soil and fertiliser while everyday waste will be sorted and recycled.

But, as breathtaking and bold as Masdar City undoubtedly is, one fact is clear, its designers and engineers are not bound by the usual set of rules and constraints. Strong political leadership twinned with generous funds means the new eco-city can showcase unorthodox innovations that the rest of the cash-strapped world would probably write off as 'pie-in-the-sky'.

So while Dongtan, and indeed Masdar City, sound like the kind of places you might like to live, could you afford it? Planned eco-cities have already been pessimistically labelled mere playgrounds for the rich. Not so, says Wood.

Pointing to the Palm in Dubai, three palm-shaped man-made islands currently under construction in the Persian Gulf, he asserts: 'The emphasis here has been to create housing for those who can afford it – the wealthy basically. This doesn't give you a city, it gives you a development of a specific resident that can afford to live there. [Eco-cities] want a mixed community, that's how cities evolve.'

And, as Wood points out ironically, this requires governance and policies, the very things Dongtan desperately needs to get started.

So as Dongtan waits for its permits, and Masdar breaks ground, architects worldwide are already designing the next wave of eco-cities. Inspired by new renewable technologies and driven by the threat of climate change, the designs include floating lilypad-style cities to house climate change refugees, urban life in houses grown from trees and a metropolis comprising high rise, algae-growing apartments […].

In late 2007, when plans for Masdar City emerged, chief executive, Sultan Al Jaber said: 'One day all cities will be like this.' Roger Wood, architects and engineers worldwide would probably beg to differ.

Welcome to Eco-city

Ian Taylor

BBC Focus, December 2008

[…]

'If you plan your development so people can live, work and shop very locally, you can quite significantly reduce the amount of energy that is used,' Wood says. 'Then, not only have you made the situation easier because you've reduced the energy demand, but it also means that producing it from renewable sources becomes easier because you don't have to produce quite so much.'

That's a big cornerstone of Arup's design for Dongtan. The aim is that the city will require 66 per cent less energy than a conventional development, with wind turbines

and solar panels complementing some 40 per cent that comes from biological sources. These include human sewage and municipal waste, both of which will be collected for energy recovery and composting. Meanwhile, a combined heat and power plant will burn waste rice husks.

We didn't want to use crops grown specifically to be used as fuel because that increases the footprint of the whole development,' Wood says. 'So we looked for a waste product.' It didn't take developers long to realise that the rice husk is one of the most plentiful waste products available in the Yangtze Delta. Although burning the husks for energy means releasing the CO_2 they absorbed as they grew, the CO_2 will be captured and fed into greenhouses to make local agriculture more efficient. 'This is part of what we call a virtuous circle – you look at a number of things and see how they all join together.'

Arup's integrated, holistic approach to city planning goes further still. Leftover heat from the power plant will be channelled to homes and businesses. Buildings can be made of thinner material because the electric cars on the road will be quiet, so there's less noise to drown out. Dongtan will initially see an 83 per cent reduction in waste sent to landfill compared to other cities, with the aim to reduce that to nothing over time. And more than 60 per cent of the whole site will be parks and farmland, where food is grown to feed the population.

Beyond the farms, a 3.5 km-wide buffer zone will separate the city from a delicate habitat for wildlife. The mudflats of Chongming Island are crucial to migrating birds and a large area on the seaward perimeter of Dongtan is a wetland protected by the Ramsar Convention. Wood says the habitat has been the biggest constraint on development, and something of an influence on the design.

Note from Arup (2009): Arup was commissioned by our client, property developer SIIC, to produce a masterplan and sustainability guidelines for the Dongtan project. We have now completed this work and our client originally intended to have the first phase of development completed in time for the 2010 Shanghai Expo. However, the start date for the construction of the first phase of Dongtan has been postponed. Our client has informed us that while full planning agreement for the project has been obtained, large development projects in China require a series of permissions from the Government, and we are currently waiting for these to be fully confirmed by SIIC.

How Masdar, in the United Arab Emerates, will work

Height control
Developers have set a height limit on buildings to make the most efficient use of shading and solar power.

Easy access
The city is designed so that nobody is ever more than 200 m from the nearest public transport.

Fresh air
'Green lungs' are strategically placed around the city to let in cool desert winds, pushing fresh air into the streets.

Shady streets
Tightly packed streets maximise shading, while buildings use thermal walls to keep internal temperatures down.

Building power
A solar power facility will be built first to help provide the power for the construction of the rest of the city.

Train links
Most of Masdar's main streets are clustered around a light railway line that provides a transport link to Abu-dhabi.

Clean water
A desalination plant will provide 8000 m^3 of water a day, and 60 per cent of the water used in Masdar will be recycled.

(Source: text from Taylor, 2008)

The centre of Masdar

© Foster + Partners

Masdar headquarters

The heart of the city, and one of the first buildings to be completed (in 2011), will be Masdar headquarters. Costing more than £150 million, the zero-carbon structure will be seven storeys high and combine the first residences and business. The photovoltaic roof will be built first to provide solar energy. Developers claim that this will make it the first building in the world to help power its own construction. When completed the headquarters will generate more energy than it actually uses. Here's how:

- The glass exterior of the building has a high thermal mass, meaning it expels heat while still being clear.
- Conical wind towers provide natural lighting, ventilation and cooling. Warm air is drawn up to the roof, while their wide bases house gardens.
- Rows of wind turbines will hang from underneath the main canopy.
- Solar-panel arrays on the roof will collect energy, while thermal tubes provide the building with solar-powered air-conditioning.
- Air will circulate through the building via an under-floor distribution system.
- The building is designed to use 70 per cent less water than a typical mixed-use building.

Transport and pedestrian deck

Height control with pedestrian deck   'Green lungs'

Pedestrian deck

Ground level Masdar will actually be 5.5 m in the air. Streets are all arranged on an elevated pedestrian deck, while all transport to and from the city happens underground. The design is similar to many airports, with all transport and maintenance kept away from the pedestrian level. This means roads will be free of traffic and never be dug up for new piping – that can be done from below. It also means that when rubbish is thrown into a bin, a vacuum chute could whisk it away to a central location to be sorted and recycled.

Transport

Since cars and other petrol-based vehicles are banned from the city, occupants will share a network of 'podcars' to get around. The 'personal rapid transit system' will comprise 2500 driverless, electric vehicles that make 150,000 trips a day by following sensors along a track beneath the pedestrian deck. Up to six passengers will ride in each pod: they just hop in at one of the 83 stations around the city and tap in their destination.

(Source: text from Taylor, 2008)

SAQ 3.3   The ecological principles behind eco-cities

To what extent are the following ecological principles used in the design of Dongtan and Masdar?

1   use of compactness in the design of the cities

2   encouraging diversity

3   use of resources more like ecosystems.

SAQ 3.4   Comparing and contrasting eco-cities

Compare and contrast the following two aspects of the planning and design of Dongtan and Masdar:

1   Who is involved in the planning of the eco-cities?

2   How are the two cities adapted to their local environment?

 Finally, watch the short video 'Eco-cities' on the course DVD. It covers similar ground to the articles you have just read, focusing on some of the thinking behind the design of Dongtan eco-city. But there is also discussion of 'retrofitting' eco-design to existing cities, and the two approaches are compared.

SAQ 3.5   Eco-cities or redesigned cities?

What are the arguments made in the video for building new eco-cities and for redesigning existing cities? Which approach is more important at the moment and why?

Dongtan was planned to start its life on a modest scale, with a community of 5000. The plan was to expand to 80 000 by 2020 and half a million by 2050 on an area of 30 km². This plan has now been scaled back; indeed, the project may not now happen. Masdar will occupy an area of 6.5 km² and have a population of 50 000 including 40 000 residents.

Both are designed to have residential areas for all the population and businesses to provide local employment for most. Interestingly, both plan to have university presences, which would attract a more adventurous population. However, although living conditions and lifestyles and the mix of population have been thought about carefully there are no inhabitants to be consulted; they will be presented with the new city and its facilities and will have to adapt to it and it to them. One criticism put forward is that they will not be realistic places for people on low incomes to live in; a possibility is that if they become popular places to live they could become the preserve of the affluent.

Both cities are designed as showcases and 'living laboratories'. They certainly make full use of ecological principles in their design and if they work according to plan they will achieve considerable savings in the use of resources and production of waste (but not complete energy or resource recycling). However, they are more test beds for future cities than finished blueprints, spaces for trying out new ideas, new structures and new technologies and for exploring how people respond to and make use of these new environments. Their main role may be to inspire and energise the ecological renewal of our current cities, helping to develop what Girardet has described in the introduction as a culture of sustainability. The next section looks at one area that may make a contribution towards this aim.

2.2   Greening the city

In contrast to the integrated approach of the eco-city, this section looks at one particular aspect of improving urban environments, that of moving to greener, lower-impact cities. It looks specifically at the potential for urban *green spaces*: the use of urban parks and urban corridors for wildlife, but also less conventional ideas, from green roofs to rooftop gardens and 'vertical' farms. My intention here is introduce some of these ideas to give you an opportunity to assess how they might help cities *adapt* to future climate change by reducing the potential impacts of flooding, heatwaves and air pollution, while providing more space for biodiversity and locally grown food and recreation for city dwellers. Greening the city in a literal sense can provide many benefits and surprisingly few drawbacks. As you read through these examples, make notes on their possible benefits; you will be asked in Section 3 to assess their impact.

Most people are familiar with parks and gardens in towns and cities, and most major urban areas have at least some green spaces. In addition, many urban residential areas also have their own green spaces or gardens, either publicly or privately owned.

Activity 3.2   Advantages of green spaces

Think of a green space you are familiar with, a park or garden for example. Make a list of the benefits you think it offers.

Discussion

Your answer will depend on your individual circumstances and interests as well as the green space you have in mind.

Here is a list I made, thinking about a large local park in London near where I live, which may include several points you have thought of.

Green spaces and gardens clearly provide space and habitats for biodiversity to flourish. They are also an important space for people. They provide aesthetic pleasure – enjoying the scenery – and a social space to relax, walking the dog or sitting with your friends and family on a sunny day, or attending an outdoor event. They also offer space for sport and exercise, for individuals and teams, from running and cycling to football and other ball games. In short they can provide us with physical, social and psychological benefits.

You may well have thought of other benefits. The social benefits are spelt out by the UK Department of Communities and Local Government, which also points out that well-planned and maintained green spaces can help regenerate run-down areas (Department of Communities and Local Government, 2009):

> Good quality, well-designed parks and green spaces make a critical contribution to our neighbourhoods, towns and cities and to people's quality of life and play an important role in creating a sense of place [...] Quality green spaces have been shown to:

- support the local economy, making neighbourhoods more desirable
- enhance physical and mental health
- benefit children and young people
- reduce crime and fear of crime
- support social cohesion
- aid movement between other spaces
- protect biodiversity and enhance the environment.

The environmental benefits are described in more detail by this excerpt from the Greater London Authority:

> Potential functions for green spaces and vegetation within the city:

- supporting biodiversity
- reducing flood risk by absorbing and temporarily retaining rainfall
- moderating the temperature through offsetting the urban heat island effect
- reducing energy demand by providing shade and reducing windspeeds
- helping to reduce noise and air pollution
- providing places for recreational and leisure activities that improve health.

(Mayor of London, 2008)

Both lists contain many more benefits than I gave in my answer to Activity 3.2. In fact they spell out many of the ecosystem services provided by green spaces to an urban population.

Are there many drawbacks to providing green spaces? Probably not too many – recall that ecosystem services are the *free* goods and services provided by healthy ecosystems and biodiversity. The maintenance of green spaces in urban areas costs money, though it also provides employment for people. Also, if green spaces are neglected they can become an eyesore and become places that feel unsafe to enjoy. However, a major reason why green spaces have been undervalued in the past is that they are often worth more in monetary terms if they are sold as land for development. But this is to pitch large gains for a few (developers and property owners, sometimes people seeking housing) against smaller benefits for many more local people. It is often the role of local government to balance these competing demands.

From this brief discussion, then, it appears that green spaces have an important role to play in cities, and should not be seen as an optional extra. In addition to their direct benefits to human welfare and support for biodiversity, they can help cities adapt to climate change by helping them to keep cool and by absorbing rainfall (see Box 3.1). Adaptation to climate change and the urban heat island are discussed in Section 3.

Box 3.1   The urban air conditioner (in praise of the urban tree)

Shade

Trees have often been planted in town and village centres to provide shade. This remains an important function in modern cities, where it can be hard to find shade, particularly as climates get warmer. However, urban trees provide a range of other important services free of charge.

Wind management

Trees are particularly good at providing protection from strong winds. All tall obstacles tend to reduce the average wind speed near the ground, but high buildings often cause very gusty conditions and divert strong winds along wind corridors. Trees, in contrast, slow winds down gently *and* reduce the strength of gusts by allowing the air to pass through their branches.

Rainfall management

All vegetation requires water to stay healthy and grow, and the soil they grow in absorbs heavy rainfall well as long as it is not compacted. Urban trees with their network of deep roots are particularly good at tapping into soil moisture and in absorbing heavy rainfall quickly. By doing this they prevent flooding in urban areas.

Supporting biodiversity

Urban trees provide habitats for a very wide range of biodiversity, from birds to invertebrates. They are also a significant source of pollen for bees in urban areas.

Air conditioner and air filter

Perhaps the most important role of trees in urban areas is their ability to cool their surroundings and remove pollutants from the air.

Trees act as *air conditioners* by cooling and humidifying their surroundings, particularly during the day and in hot, sunny weather when the cooling is most needed. A large tree will take up to 1000 litres of water a day from its roots to be used in photosynthesis and transport nutrients to its growing tips. To maintain this circulation the water is evaporated from tiny pores in its leaves. This process of evaporation in growing plants is called transpiration and was described in Block 3. It has a strong cooling effect on the local environment. The evaporation of 1000 litres of water absorbs over 600 kWh of energy from the surroundings, equivalent to running dozens of air conditioners.

Trees also act as *air filters*. Although they can be damaged, as people are, by air pollution, they are efficient at removing pollutants such as sulphur dioxide, nitrogen dioxide and ozone. They do this by absorbing these gases in the normal process of taking in air to obtain oxygen for photosynthesis and then breaking down these other chemicals into less harmful ones. They also trap damaging air pollution in the form of small solid or liquid particles on their leaves and other surfaces, which are then flushed away by the next heavy rainfall or fall to the ground when leaves drop (Scheer, 2001).

Economic and aesthetic value

Trees often have a high value in urban areas, which means that it is viable for them to be managed sustainably while any waste products such as trimmings and cuttings can be used and recycled.

Costs

Ideally, there should be 'cradle to grave' management of trees in urban areas: from planting new trees, keeping them healthy and safe, to tree surgery of dangerous branches or of dead or dying trees at the end of their lives. This regular maintenance costs money.

Trees can cause damage or injury from falling branches or if the whole tree falls. Tree roots can also cause subsidence in clay areas by extracting water from the ground and causing it to shrink. This occurs only if trees are planted too close to buildings or allowed to grow too large and depends on the type of tree. Finally, some birds roosting in trees and some insects feeding on trees, cause droppings of various messy organic materials that are not always popular with owners of cars who park underneath. Common sense and proper maintenance and care with planting of trees, avoids the majority of these problems.

Parks and gardens may be the most commonly encountered green spaces in cities, but they are not the only form that green spaces can take. With an increased awareness of their benefits has come a renewed interest in other forms of greenery, some reviving old traditions, some hi-tech and exotic.

144

Green corridors (Figure 3.3) are not a new idea; they have been discussed in the context of providing corridors for animals and plants to move along, to allow them to migrate between separated habitats or refuges, and more recently in the context of climate change. There is now a similar interest in developing and maintaining green corridors in urban areas for use by people as well as wildlife. The case for green corridors is made in the following quote from a local authority action plan:

> Green corridors are linear features of mostly open character, including canal towpaths, riverside paths, footpaths, cycleways and bridleways, which act as wildlife corridors and attractive, safe off-road links between residential areas,

(a)   (b)

(c)

Figure 3.3 (a) an urban park; (b) a row of urban trees; (c) a green corridor

open spaces, urban centres, leisure facilities and employment areas. They also give residents access to natural green space and the open countryside and provide opportunities for recreation. Green corridors increase in value if they are linked to form a network that extends within and beyond the borough boundary.

Local networks of high quality and well-managed and maintained open spaces, sport and recreational facilities help create urban environments that are attractive, clean and safe.

(Broxbourne, 2008)

Here the focus is on value to local residents and creating a clean and attractive urban environment. Note that green corridors refer to waterways, rivers and canals as well as footpaths and tracks. Green corridors also have another role: properly sited, they can help to channel clean and cool air into cities from the surrounding countryside.

SAQ 3.6   Assessing green spaces

Use your understanding of the environmental, social and economic dimensions of sustainability to make a rough assessment of the contribution that green spaces and corridors can make towards a sustainable city.

Another, more novel form of greening cities is the development of what are sometimes called *vertical habitats*. This term means the encouragement or creation of living (green) areas amongst the three-dimensional space of urban architecture, often, but not always, on tall buildings, and sometimes on its vertical spaces. It includes developments such as green roofs, green walls (or vertical gardens) and vertical farms.

Green roofs are not new. Using turf as a cover for roofs has long been a tradition in many wet or cold countries because it helps to keep out the rain and provides good insulation in winter (Figure 3.4). Many businesses and authorities are now looking again at this ancient practice and reassessing the advantages and disadvantages of building green roofs. Fitting green roofs to existing buildings or designing green roofs for new buildings is expensive because the roof is heavy and needs extra structural support; it is mainly suited to flat roofs and it needs regular maintenance.

The advantages, like those of green spaces, are surprisingly numerous, as this summary from an organisation that promotes green roofs and living roofs in the UK claims:

Reduction of Urban Heat Island – Research in Tyndall Centre for Climate Change suggests we need a 10% increase in green space in our cities to combat climate change. This is particularly relevant to the reduction in the Urban Heat Island effect [in larger urban areas]. Green roofs are recognized to have a positive effect on reducing [this effect].

(a)

(b)

Figure 3.4 Green roofs: (a) traditional Nordic huts, Faroe Islands; (b) modern example, Chicago

Biodiversity – Green roofs can provide important refuges for wildlife in urban areas. Research in Switzerland and the UK has demonstrated that green roofs can provide important refuges for rare invertebrate populations.

Water – Green roofs can significantly reduce the surface run off volumes and rates of rainfall leaving roofs. […] Green roofs can help reduce flash floods as a consequence of intense rainfall events. This will become increasingly important as a consequence of climate change.

Green roofs also improve the quality of water and although the amount of water is reduced it is possible to harvest rainfall from roofs that have been greened.

Thermal Performance – Green roofs cannot be given a U-value [insulation rating] at present. However they have been shown to significantly reduce the need for air conditioning in summer and can provide a degree of insulation in winter.

Sound Insulation – The combination of soil, plants and trapped layers of air within green roof systems can act as a sound insulation barrier. Sound waves are absorbed, reflected or deflected. The growing medium tends to block lower sound frequencies whilst the plants block higher frequencies.

Protection of Waterproofing – The original green roofs in Germany stem from covering wet bitumen with 6 cm of sand, which became vegetated. This covering was to protect the wet bitumen from fire. Green roofs have now been shown to double if not triple the life of waterproofing membranes beneath the green roof.

Air Quality – airborne particles and pollutants are filtered from the atmosphere by the substrates and vegetation on a green roof.

Amenity Space – in dense urban environments there is often a lack of green space for residents. Roof Gardens and roof top parks provide important green spaces to improve the quality of life for urban residents.

(Green Roof Consultancy, n.d.)

As with other green spaces, green roofs can benefit more than their owners or the people who live in their buildings, which is another reason why city and local authorities, Dongtan for example (Warren, 2009), are beginning to encourage them.

Activity 3.3   How green roofs benefit more than their owners

The previous paragraph mentioned that green roofs 'benefit more than their owners'. Describe in your own words what you think this means.

Discussion

Some of the advantages listed here apply only to the residents of the host building, for example improved sound insulation, but others have a wider impact on the urban environment. Green roofs help to reduce surface run-off from rainstorms, reducing flooding and the need for flood prevention schemes, and can provide unusual habitats to encourage rare species. Along with other green spaces they can improve air quality and help to reduce the urban heat island effect. Although these effects may be quite modest, they benefit the whole urban community. This is an example of a positive externality (look back at Block 5, Part 3, Box 3.1 if you need to remind yourself about this).

Green walls or vertical gardens are certainly not a new concept; mosses and wild plants are attracted naturally to damp walls and railway cuttings, while the sides of many houses are decorated with climbing plants. However, designs of green walls for modern buildings, which rely on lightweight support systems and careful watering systems, have now become fashionable, but while interesting as artistic statements (Figure 3.5), they seem unlikely to make a major contribution to sustainable urban living.

(a)   (b)

Figure 3.5 (a) Green walls; (b) a design for a vertical farm

Vertical gardens: The height of fashion

First conceived in the aquarium of an earnest French schoolboy in the 1960s, it is now invading our cities like some green thing from a science-fiction movie. It climbs up shopping malls in Seoul and Thailand, galleries and museums in Paris and Madrid and Kanazawa, Japan. It appears in restaurants in Shanghai and Los Angeles, and in a concert hall in Taipei.

It has become an emblem of contemporary France, to be installed in the country's embassies. It has received the indispensable imprimatur of Stella McCartney, who used one in her catwalk show in 2007, and is about to make its most conspicuous appearances to date in London, on the five-star Athenaeum Hotel in Piccadilly, and on The Driver, a pub-turned-exclusive-club in King's Cross.

It has become an essential accessory of luxury apartments, and it has reached the point of diffusion to a mass market: a company called VertiGarden has leapt on the bandwagon with a more homespun system of hanging baskets, which you can whack up on your own back wall.

The appeal is easy to understand. It's hard to hate a plant, and at one level the Vertical Garden is a simply an upgrade on the palms and rubber plants with which companies and individuals have long tried to enliven their hard-edged environments. It also catches the ecological spirit of the age.

It would, in fact, take an awful lot of Vertical Gardens to make much difference to the world's CO_2 but they are still a charming way for the environmentally conscious to wear their green on their sleeve.

The Vertical Garden, or Le Mur Vegetal, is the invention of 56-year-old French botanist Patrick Blanc, who is responsible for the installations on the Athenaeum and The Driver.

(Moore, 2009)

At first sight, the idea of **vertical farms** seems as unlikely as vertical gardens, but they may be a more practical proposition. Urban farming is as old as cities themselves, although it has tended to migrate to the surrounding countryside. It is also built into the design for both Dongtan and Masdar. In recent decades, however, as agriculture and the food and drinks industries have become global businesses, it is less common for food to be grown close to where it is consumed.

The basic idea of 'vertical farming' is that cities should be able to grow most of their food inside their boundaries by using highly efficient greenhouse culture. The proponents point out that 'well-designed greenhouses use as little as 10% of the water and 5% of the area required by farm fields' (Vogel, 2008). Examples of a simple approach would be the use of rooftop greenhouses and floating greenhouses (for example, barges floating on rivers) to grow fruit and vegetables. Rooftop greenhouses have the advantage of a ready supply of underfloor heating, while floating greenhouses have a ready supply of water. Both grow food close to where it will be consumed.

A more ambitious alternative is the truly vertical farm that makes use of the vertical surfaces of office buildings to grow crops, and could be adapted to modern building designs:

Double-glass facades are already popular among architects as an energy-saver, allowing winter sun in while insulating against noise and heat loss. In the summer, most double facades have built-in shades to keep the interior cool. Hydroponic gardens [growing plants in water rather than soil] could provide the shade.

(Vogel, 2008)

This approach would be much more expensive initially, but if heat and lighting came from renewable sources and nitrogen and other nutrients were recycled from animals or the sewage system, then the environmental impact would be very low.

Activity 3.4   The case for vertical farming

What are the environmental arguments in favour of vertical farming?

Discussion

Vertical farming can be thought of as a new form of urban farming that makes use of the structures of modern buildings. In addition to the traditional advantage of producing high-value food such as fruit close to its consumers is the use of farming methods (glasshouses and hydroponics) that make good use of space and water, while reusing heat from the buildings and nutrients from city wastes. The environmental case is good, but needs to be balanced against the high cost of some initiatives and novel technologies that still need developing.

Summary of Section 2

The study of London's public transport 100 years ago illustrates that the infrastructure of major cities is continually changing – it is possible to imagine urban areas based on ecological principles rather than economic development that would be radically different while still meeting the needs of inhabitants. Eco-cities represent a dramatic way to re-imagine the shape of the city of the future and to try out ecological measures that may be adopted by existing cities.

Urban green spaces come in a variety of forms, from traditional parks and gardens and 'green corridors' to more experimental 'vertical habitats' such as green roofs or vertical farms that make use of the vertical dimensions of modern cities. Their value to urban environments can be assessed in terms of their economic, social and environmental contribution. Whatever their forms, urban green spaces provide a range of valuable environmental services and economic and social benefits to city dwellers for very little cost.

3 The changing city

Cities face many challenges this century from migration and rapid population growth, poverty and affluence, and the disruptive pressures of globalisation and new technologies. In addition, they now have to respond to environmental change, globally and locally, by reducing their own environmental impacts and by preparing for changes resulting from climate change. Growing environmental pressures from climate change include water shortages, rising sea levels and threats to food security which will, in turn, add to the demands on cities. They will, for example, have to support and provide livelihoods for unknown numbers of environmental refugees. This adds urgency to plans to develop 'healthy' cities that can adapt to environmental change and reduce their vulnerabilities to floods and other threats. Cities are not just eco-villains; they can have positive roles to play in creating living spaces for more people and encouraging biodiversity.

Section 2 explored how cities can become places that are good to live in by reducing their environmental impacts and bringing green spaces and biodiversity back into the city. This section continues these themes in exploring how cities can adapt to environmental change. It looks at two examples of how London is responding to the growing threats from climate change that affect many urban areas of the world, heatwaves and floods, and follows with a third example of how biodiversity is adapting to urban life.

3.1   Adapting to climate change

Climate change will affect all of us in future decades through its global impacts on water and on food security. Changing patterns of rainfall, increasing temperatures plus extreme events such as heatwaves, floods and drought will affect most of the world's ecosystems and put the wellbeing and health of billions of people at risk (Costello, 2009). Healthy cities have to maintain healthy populations but, as Part 1 has shown, this does not always happen. The next section focuses specifically on a growing health risk to populations in cool temperate climates like those of western Europe.

3.1.1   Heatwaves in the city

This section explores the high mortality rate of vulnerable people in Europe and the UK during a heatwave that occurred in the hot summer of 2003. It asks why people in large cities were particularly vulnerable and what can be done to avoid similar problems in the future. Box 3.2 describes what happened.

Box 3.2   The European heatwave of 2003

In 2003 Western Europe experienced its hottest summer ever recorded. Although climate change was not the cause of the extreme heat it almost certainly added to its intensity. It provides a taste of what global warming will mean to Europe and the UK in future decades. The summer temperature exceeded the 1961–1990 average by 2.3 °C and the months of June and August were particularly hot. In particular, the heatwave in the first two weeks of August led to considerably more deaths in western Europe than would be expected in summer. The excess deaths were concentrated in major cities like Paris, where approximately 20,000 died causing an enormous political storm. England and Wales were also affected by unusual heat and more than 2000 deaths have been attributed to this one event between 4th and 13th August (Kovats et al., 2005). Southern and eastern England were worst hit and 600 deaths were recorded in London. These were the worst peacetime fatalities in the UK since the great London smog of 1952, but surprisingly drew very little comment from the British press. The elderly were most badly affected; deaths of those over 75 years old were one-third more than usual (Kovats et al., 2005), but other vulnerable adults also suffered because the heat was also accompanied by high levels of air pollution. Figure 3.6 illustrates the excess deaths that occurred in London; it shows a very similar pattern to the excess deaths of the Great Smog of 1952 shown in Part 1. But this time many of the deaths were preventable and quite a few took place in care homes.

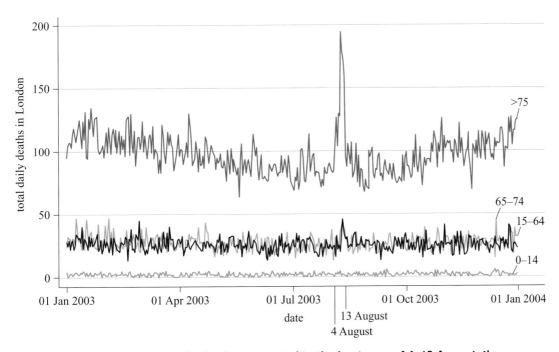

Figure 3.6 The abnormal peak in deaths connected to the heatwave of 4–13 August; the numbers on the right refer to the age of those affected *(Source: redrawn from Mayor of London, 2006)*

Why were the populations of cities like London and Paris particularly vulnerable to a heatwave? The elderly are more at risk from overheating because they are less able to maintain their temperatures (they are also more at risk from cold) and are less likely to notice that this control is not working. The critical physiological factor appears to be that people who get overheated during the day can usually recover if they can cool off at night, but are in trouble if they cannot. During a heatwave, high night-time temperatures can cause more harm than high daytime temperatures.

Activity 3.5   Too hot for comfort

Why might living in a city or large town put people, particularly the elderly, more at risk from heatwaves?

Discussion

Several social factors come to mind. Cities are home to large numbers of people who live in relative poverty and often in poor housing. More generally, the types of urban housing that people live in – high-rise flats for example – may become hotter or there may be fewer cooler rooms than in older or larger houses. It may be less easy for the elderly to reach a cool, safe place outside, such as a garden. Also, many urban elderly do not have family living nearby and may not have friends or neighbours who visit regularly.

In addition, the centres of towns and cities are warmer than the surrounding countryside, particularly at night. Air pollution may also be a factor, although pollution levels today can be as high in the country as in towns.

Lack of social support networks or even basic information, the awareness that there is a problem, is one factor. The nature of our housing stock in the UK is another – our houses and flats have been designed to keep out wind and rain and to keep people warm (often poorly), not to keep them cool.

The other factor discussed in Activity 3.5, the extra warmth in cities and towns, is known as the urban heat island effect, or UHI, and has several causes:

- The vertical structure of cities and towns means that they behave somewhat like canyons in desert areas. Cooling winds and convection are reduced, slowing the transfer of heat away from built-up areas.

- Heat is emitted directly from the large numbers of homes, workplaces and vehicles into comparatively small areas.

- Heat is absorbed during the day by materials such as the concrete of buildings and road surfaces and then released during the night.

- Urban areas dry out quickly – most rain runs off quickly into drains – and have few green areas. This means that less heat is lost by evaporation or transpiration by plants than in the countryside.

The net effect is to increase the temperature in the centre of cities with respect to the surrounding countryside. The urban heat island generally increases with the size of the city and is most apparent on clear and calm days and nights, particularly at night. These, of course, are exactly the conditions that occur in hot weather. In London on clear, calm summer nights the temperature in the centre of town is typically 6 °C warmer than in the surrounding countryside, as Figure 3.7 shows. The cooler area in the bottom left shows the cooling effect of London's largest area of green space, Richmond Park.

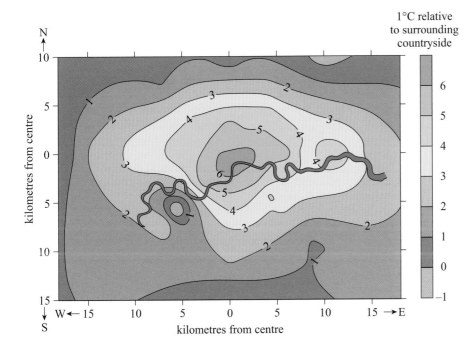

Figure 3.7 Air temperature of London's heat island under calm and dry conditions for six nights (2–3 a.m.) during the summer of 2000 (Source: redrawn from Mayor of London, 2006)

The night-time temperatures experienced across London on 7 August 2003 are illustrated in fine detail by Figure 3.8, taken by an infrared satellite camera. The increase in temperature towards the centre of London is clear, and the cooler areas on the fringes of the map are found near woodlands, parks or lakes.

A complicating factor in this story is air pollution. The air above the UK and particularly over towns is much cleaner than in the 1950s when the Great Smog (described in Part 1) occurred. Those kinds of winter smog still occur today but much less often and, because of the cleaner air, towns across Britain now get much more sunshine in winter than 50 or 100 years ago. However, a different kind of air pollution is now common, first noted in sunny cities like Los Angeles. It is associated with dry, hot days in spring and summer rather than in winter. The main pollutants of summer smog are ozone, nitrogen dioxides and particulates and the main cause is now emissions from cars, lorries and other forms of transport that burn fossil

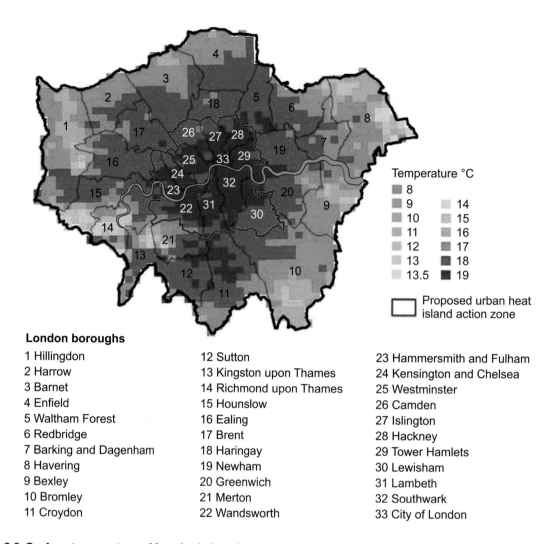

London boroughs

1 Hillingdon	12 Sutton	23 Hammersmith and Fulham
2 Harrow	13 Kingston upon Thames	24 Kensington and Chelsea
3 Barnet	14 Richmond upon Thames	25 Westminster
4 Enfield	15 Hounslow	26 Camden
5 Waltham Forest	16 Ealing	27 Islington
6 Redbridge	17 Brent	28 Hackney
7 Barking and Dagenham	18 Haringay	29 Tower Hamlets
8 Havering	19 Newham	30 Lewisham
9 Bexley	20 Greenwich	31 Lambeth
10 Bromley	21 Merton	32 Southwark
11 Croydon	22 Wandsworth	33 City of London

Figure 3.8 Surface temperature of London's heat island measured by satellite infrared cameras during the August 2003 heatwave. Note that this is the Greater London area as shown in Figure 1.37. *(Source: adapted from Mayor of London, 2008)*

fuels. Ozone is produced when the chemical emissions react in sunlight and in warm weather. But the process takes several hours, and because the air is usually moving, ozone is often found across large areas of the country and not just in towns. Today, the most damaging pollution episodes occur during hot, dry, sunny weather and often accompany heatwaves.

What can be done to avert future tragedies? Heat events will occur more frequently in the future because of global warming, but simple steps have been taken by government agencies to ensure that suitable information is available and the right social support networks are in place. Many of the actions needed to protect vulnerable populations are extremely basic – checking that they are drinking enough water and taking them to a cool place if they have become heat stressed. It is shameful that many care homes did not understand this. The UK Department of Health has published an advisory booklet that is sent to all relevant NHS units, local authorities and social services and care home providers with advice on the effects of heat, who is affected and what can be done (Department of Health, 2009). At its core is a four-level system of preparedness outlining the responsibilities of each agency:

- Level 1 Summer – preparedness at national, regional and local level, including information for the general public and long-term planning.
- Level 2 Alert and readiness stage is triggered by a warning from the Meteorological Office, a 'heat-health watch'.
- Level 3 Heatwave action stage is triggered when threshold temperatures have been reached in any region.
- Level 4 Emergency stage is triggered when a heatwave is so severe or prolonged that power or water shortages occur and the integrity of health and social care systems is threatened.

The UK Meteorological Office now operates a heat-health watch system for England and Wales, run in association with the Department of Health and the Welsh Assembly, and issues Level 2, 3 and 4 warnings of dangerously hot weather every summer when circumstances arise.

What of the longer term? The Department of Health booklet gives useful information on action that can be taken by individuals, health care organisations and other agencies to plan for the longer term at the local level. It includes greening the built environment, shading and insulating housing and buildings (against heat and cold) and measures to reduce carbon emissions. The department gives specific advice for hospitals and care homes on measures to assist cooling without using air conditioning.

The Greater London Authority has also responded by looking at the planning for London as a whole to reduce the impacts of future heatwaves. The London climate change adaptation strategy (Mayor of London, 2008) suggests a set of priority actions:

- Lead an 'urban greening programme' to cool the city using green spaces, street trees and urban design.
- Create an 'Urban Heat Island Action Area' where new development must contribute to cooling the city.
- Enhance Londoners' access to cool buildings during heatwaves to help people recover.
- Provide London-specific design guidance to enable architects to reduce the risk of new development overheating in future summers.

SAQ 3.7   Measures to avoid heatwaves

1   Why do you think advice was given on cooling without using air conditioning?

2   How might an 'urban greening programme' cool a city?

3   Make a list of other, longer-term measures that could be used to avoid heatwaves and their effects.

What lessons can be drawn from this short study of the health impacts of a recent heatwave? The first is that *adaptation of behaviour* can be simple and effective in countries where strong institutions are in place. Well-organised government and community responses to a perceived threat can change individual and organisational behaviour by providing helpful information and timely warnings. The second is that cities and towns will have to *adapt* their urban environment to prepare for changes to come, but in ways that *reduce* resource and energy use so they do not add to global warming. This is likely to be more challenging, but a first step can be made by changing the priorities of organisations at local and regional scales. Local communities can do this for themselves. Any longer-term responses will have to be sustainable for many decades and are likely to be much more difficult to get right and more costly to achieve. Most buildings in UK cities, for example, are not designed to cope with hot weather and need to be adapted. But any adaptations, local or city wide, would have to remain flexible and responsive to future change. They would, in effect, become part of the changes towards building sustainable cities, no doubt using many of the ideas and principles of eco-cities discussed earlier.

This example suggests that cities and countries can adapt and learn from disasters if they have the organisational capacity, and that while some actions are comparatively easy to make, others are less so and may demand greater political will and public support. They will need to. According to the UK Meteorological Office:

> In the future, extreme heatwave events similar to that seen in 2003 are likely to become more frequent because of continued man-made climate change. Using a climate model simulation [based on continued medium to high CO_2 emissions] we predict that more than half of all European summers are likely to be warmer than that of 2003 by the 2040s, and by the 2060s a 2003-type summer would be unusually cool.

(Hadley Centre, 2004)

A more recent study by the UK Climate Impacts Programme puts some figures on the expected temperature rises for the UK by the 2080s *if emissions are not controlled over this coming century*. The UK, it should be noted, will not be hit as hard as most of mainland Europe by climate change.

All areas of the UK warm, more so in summer than in winter. Changes in summer mean temperatures are greatest in parts of southern England (up to 4.2 °C (2.2 to 6.8 °C)) and least in the Scottish islands (just over 2.5 °C (1.2 to 4.1 °C)).

(Jenkins et al., 2009

These temperature rises and the changes shown in Figure 3.9 are based on what the United Kingdom Climate Impacts Programme calls 'central estimates' of changing climate for the UK. They represent the mid-range of what can be expected for a 'moderate' scenario of greenhouse gas emissions. The range of uncertainty, shown in the quoted numbers, is large so this information is best treated as a guide to what might occur if no action is taken. It does not include either the most optimistic or the worst-case scenarios.

The central estimates quoted and illustrated in Figure 3.9(c) show that by the 2080s summer temperatures across the whole UK will be more than 3 °C higher than they are now, ranging from a difference of 2.5 °C in the north of Scotland to over 4 °C in southern England. By then a 2003-type summer with its damaging heatwave, with an excess of 2.3 °C, will indeed be unusually cool. Figures 3.9 (a) and (b) also present the central estimates of changes expected in precipitation (snow and rainfall). Broadly speaking, UK winters are expected to get wetter while summers become drier, with the trends being larger in the south than the north of the country. The uncertainty attached to these estimates is again very high, but the trends can provide a context for the discussion in the following section.

3.1.2   That sinking feeling

Ever since the first cities were built near rivers and oceans they have had to coexist with the seasonal flooding from rivers and the storms of the rainy seasons. Today, larger populations than ever before across the globe, including many in cities, are vulnerable to floods in spite of the many defences that have been built on coasts and rivers. They risk losing their lives, their livelihoods or their homes to floods. There are many reasons for this, but the most important is simply the great increase in numbers of people living in low-lying areas near the coast or by rivers. Certain areas such as fertile deltas in parts of Asia, where tropical storms are common, have always been prone to sudden inundation and large loss of life. But many major cities are also sited near rivers and coasts and their large populations are also at risk. This includes the cities of affluent countries, as the flooding of New Orleans demonstrated in 2005 when its flood defences were overwhelmed by Hurricane Katrina.

In recent decades, pressures from environmental changes have added to the prevailing risks from floods in many parts of the planet. These include:

- deforestation of steep-sided hills leading to increased run-off into rivers and mud slides
- removal or damage to mangrove forests, coral reefs and coastal wetlands, which provide natural protection from flooding

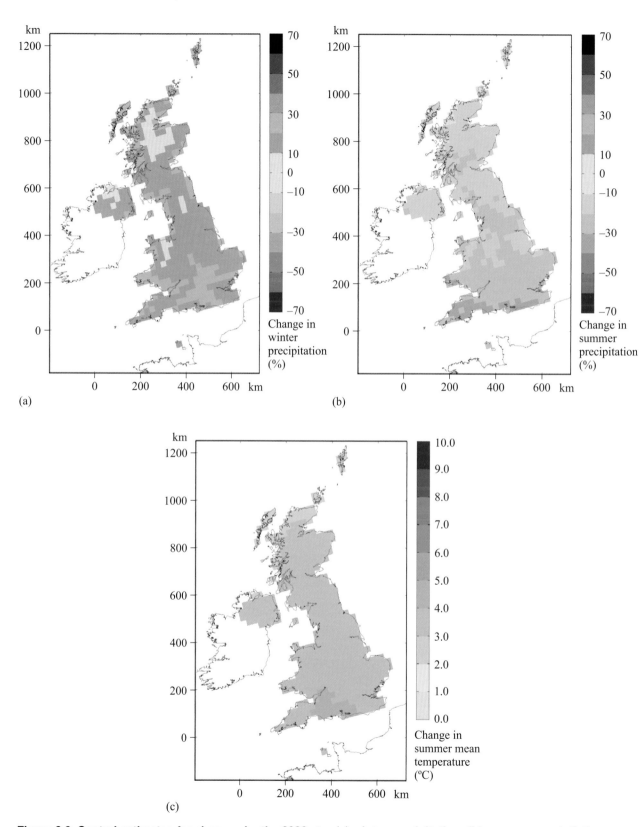

Figure 3.9 Central estimates for changes by the 2080s to: (a) winter precipitation; (b) summer precipitation (c) summer mean temperatures *(Source: redrawn from UK* **Climate Projections, 2009)**

- changes to river channels to speed up flow or allow river transport, and draining of flood plains for use by agriculture or for building
- the sinking of delta areas no longer replenished by seasonal flooding, where flood controls or water extraction are in place
- changes to the intensity and seasonal patterns of storms and storm paths of both tropical storms (hurricanes and cyclones) and temperate weather systems (depressions)
- retreat of glaciers and seasonal snow packs which store winter precipitation in the form of snow and ice and release it during summer
- steady rise in global sea level, which increases the flood risks of global communities.

Climate change is the major contributor to the last three pressures.

Moving closer to home in the UK, not all of these factors apply, but there is an additional factor that has contributed to many recent floods (and this also applies elsewhere). This is the paving over of urban areas, leading to increased run-off during storms, which is exacerbated when the buildings are on river flood plains (see Figure 3.10).

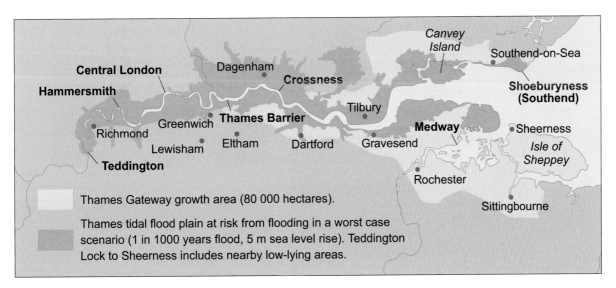

Figure 3.10 Flood map of the Thames region, including areas at risk from flooding (Source: adapted from Environment Agency, 2009)

In the UK three main categories of flooding can be identified:

1 Flooding from the sea, which usually occurs when high tides coincide with storms. When the winds from the storm drive a large mass of water towards the coast at high tide, usually over a period of several hours, this is known as a 'tidal' surge. A notable one occurred in

January 1953, when many ships were lost around the coast of the British Isles and large parts of the Low Countries, eastern England and the Thames Estuary were inundated, leading to substantial loss of life. The Thames Barrier (Figure 3.11), along with many other sea defences, was built to protect the east and south-east of England from future tidal surges.

2   River or fluvial flooding. This can be in the form of 'flash floods', when heavy rain from a local downpour falls in a few hours over the catchment of a small, steep-sloping river basin. Or it can come

(a)

(b)

(c)

(d)

Figure 3.11 Flooding and defences: (a) Thames Barrier; (b) sea defences at Leigh-On-Sea; (c) local flooding in Tewkesbury; (d) urban surface run-off

from heavy rain over a larger area and often for a longer time so that water overflows the banks of major rivers on to their floodplains. Many of the larger rivers in the UK are prone to flooding of this kind, particularly during late autumn and winter, but also at other times of the year.

3   Surface run-off. This is a feature of urban and suburban environments and can also appear in the form of flash floods. It is rainfall-derived flooding, which occurs when heavy rain falls over any urban environment and there are not sufficient green areas for the rain to soak into. Rain runs off the hard surfaces of buildings, drives and roads and into storm drains. It either overruns the drains, leading to flooding, or the drains become overloaded and the water, often mixed with sewage, floods downstream. Either can lead to sudden local floods.

Two additional flooding categories are sometimes listed: flooding from sewers, which has been included here under surface run-off, and ground water flooding from rising water levels in aquifers, not usually a major source of floods in the UK. To see how climate change may affect the risk of flooding in your area, go to the Block 6 web resources on the course website, where you will find a link to the UK Climate Impacts Programme, mentioned in the previous section on heatwaves.

SAQ 3.8   Environment change and flooding

1   For each of the three categories of flooding, give an example of how environmental change may increase the risk of flooding.

2   What contribution can green spaces make to reducing flood risk?

Having established the types of flood risk that the affect the UK, this final part looks at how the Environment Agency, the leading government agency tasked with protecting and improving the environment in England and Wales, deals with flooding. Its work includes tackling flooding and pollution incidents, cleaning up rivers and coastal communities and improving wildlife habitats. The course DVD contains an interview with two members of the Environment Agency, Chris Burnham and Rachel Hill, who are involved in managing flood risks in the London and Thames Estuary regions. They look at the role of the Thames Barrier and discuss their approaches to managing flood risks, which includes the use of green spaces and engaging with local people. Make a note of the questions in Activity 3.6, then listen to 'Environment Agency interview' on your DVD, which will take about half an hour.

Activity 3.6   Responding to flood risks

Consider the following questions as you listen to the interview with Chris Burnham and Rachel Hill.

1 What does Rachel mean by 'good floods' and 'bad floods'?

2 What is the importance of people's attitudes to flooding and how might this change?

3 Try to summarise in a sentence or two the Environment Agency's approach to flooding.

Discussion

1 Flooding is only a problem if it ends up where it is not wanted. A 'bad flood' is water in your front room. A 'good flood' is water flooding on open spaces and agricultural lands where is brings sediments and nutrients which can be good for agriculture and biodiversity.

2 People in places such as Canvey Island, where there was great loss of life in 1953, have a siege mentality and expect large defences against flooding. People in frequently flooded areas (e.g. parts of West London) are prepared and more relaxed about regular flooding of footpaths and car parks (though not about flooding in their houses!). In the future, with increased risks from flooding, new developments that can't cope with floods should be avoided, but people should be prepared for and not fearful about 'good' flooding.

3 Rather than simply building larger and larger defences, their approach is to create areas where natural flooding can occur which helps protect people from major floods, and also to consult with local populations.

3.2   Urban biodiversity

Part of re-imagining cities is to reconnect them to the 'natural' world and possibly to learn lessons from how biodiversity adapts to changing environments, particularly urban environments. Cities are now significant providers of habitats for biodiversity, and one important, often overlooked aspect of a city is how wildlife has been and is adapting to urban environments. Cities in the western world now command more resources than ever before, but if their inhabitants do not appreciate what is in their own urban backyard, they are less likely to understand and value global biodiversity. According to this viewpoint, cities and city dwellers hold the key:

> It is particularly ironic that the battle to save the world's remaining healthy ecosystems will be won or lost not in tropical forests or coral reefs that are threatened but on the streets of the most unnatural landscapes on the planet.

> (*Worldwatch Institute, 2007*)

Most of the population of the UK live in towns or cities, and if they do not they are probably near one and visit them regularly. Even if they live in the countryside they are effectively living in environments that have been adapted to serve the needs of cities and city dwellers, whether to provide food or recreation. The same is true not only for much of Europe, but increasingly worldwide. The spread of towns and cities has also had a significant impact on biodiversity. In central Europe, for example, cities occupy about 10% of land, nearly ten times the protected areas set aside for conservation (Reichholf, 2008). Globally their direct impact in terms of land occupation is less, closer to 3%, but their influence is still felt strongly: one-quarter of all the world's protected areas are within 17 km of an urban area (Elmqvist, 2008).

In many cases urban sprawl and the spread of city boundaries is destroying or threatening habitats, including critical reservoirs rich in biodiversity in places such as southern Brazil and the Cape of South Africa. Cities are also often the entry point for invasive species, which can lead to cities across the world becoming host to a similar group of plants and animals. On the other hand, cities and their suburbs now often support a greater diversity of life than the surrounding countryside, particularly where intensive agriculture cultivates large areas of similar crops. According to Elmqvist:

> A remarkable amount of native species diversity is known to exist in and around large cities such as Singapore, Canberra, Rio de Janeiro, Chicago, Berlin, New Delhi and Stockholm.

> *(Elmqvist, 2008)*

The first national urban park in the world, in Stockholm, has the highest species richness of any area of a similar size in the whole of Sweden, while a recent study of moth diversity in Munich found that, with:

> …120 lepidoptera (moth) species in the inner city and more than 600 in the open, unused areas at the periphery, cities have a higher diversity than the agricultural land in the surroundings. Gardens and parks are well above average and certain urban districts could easily compete with the species diversity in areas of nature conservation.

> *(Reichholf, 2008)*

Activity 3.7   Urban wildlife habitats

Think about the city or town where you live, or one you are familiar with, and make a list of some urban wildlife habitats you would expect to find there.

Discussion

There are a variety of wildlife habitats you might have thought of: canals, allotments, river foreshores, the verges of railways and motorways, gardens, but also woodlands, parks and farms.

In addition, wasteland or brownfield sites – the unofficial countryside of cities – play host to a variety of early colonisers on disturbed ground, such as fireweed or rosebay willow herb, and provide habitats for a variety of species. Buildings, too, with their walls and roofs and ledges, provide undisturbed habitats for certain plants and roosts for birds and bats, just as they do in the countryside.

Cities can be a direct threat to biodiversity by spreading their physical boundaries and destroying habitats such as woods and fields that support a wide variety of biological communities. Equally, though, they can provide alternative and often more varied habitats that can lead to greater diversity (Figure 3.12).

(a)   (b)

(c)

Figure 3.12 Various urban habitats: (a) railway cutting; (b) brownfield site; (c) canal scene

3.3   London's changing biodiversity

This section explores two aspects of London's changing biodiversity.
It looks first at the significance of the River Thames and its estuary in
providing habitats for wildlife as well as resources and services to its
human inhabitants.

3.3.1   Estuary life

Like many cities in the UK and around the world, London is sited where
a sizeable river meets the sea. Rivers provide many free services that
make it easy for people to gather together in large numbers: fresh water
for drinking and agriculture, easy means of transport with links to the
oceans, ready supplies of food, even building materials and a sluice to
remove wastes. For centuries the River Thames and its estuary has been
the main artery for commerce and commodities, supplying the capital of
an important nautical power. Although today air transport now carries
far more people into and out of the capital and the south-east of England,
the Thames remains the UK's most commercially important estuary, and
the Port of London still handles 10% of the UK's trade from shipping and
serves nearly a third of the UK population (Thames Estuary Partnership,
1999). It is also a major provider of habitats to wildlife and of open space for
leisure and recreation.

- Over 12 million people live within easy reach of the estuary.
- The estuary is an internationally important area for wildlife. It supports 116
  different species of fish and its mudflats and marshes are home to 170 000
  birds.
- Nearly 300 000 water birds over-winter in the Greater Thames area, making
  it the most important estuary in the UK for birds.
- The estuary, along with the Medway and Swale estuaries, to its east, make
  up one of the busiest water recreation areas in the UK. The water's edge and
  banks of the Thames are also an important resource for anglers, wildfowlers,
  cyclists, horse riders and bird watchers.

(Thames Estuary Partnership, 1999)

In addition, London's reservoirs in north and west London also provide
habitats for birds and fish and spaces for recreation and leisure. Both the
Thames and its estuary have suffered from dumped waste and pollution for
centuries but, in recent years, significant improvements in water quality
have allowed them to support a diverse range of species again. Many of the
resources provided by the Thames and its estuary are examples of
ecosystem services.

SAQ 3.9   Ecosystem services

List the ecosystem services provided by the Thames and its estuary.

Box 3.3 gives more details of some particular habitats found along the estuary and the species they support, but it also mentions impacts from building defences against tidal flooding. Like many habitats near urban centres these are continually changing as planners try to balance demand for multiple uses in the estuary. Read through the information presented, then answer SAQ 3.10.

> ### Box 3.3   Examples of habitats and species found along the Thames estuary
>
> **Intertidal mudflats**
>
> These extend throughout the estuary and are dependent on the continual deposition of sediment at a rate at least equal to that lost through erosion and sea level rise. Widths of over 4 km occur in the outer estuary, east of Canvey Island. Their loss in the inner estuary is largely due to the construction of concrete embankments and development extending onto the foreshore. Smaller but equally valuable mudflats are found within the London urban areas. Mudflats support large numbers of invertebrates (shellfish and worms), algae and eelgrass, which provide food for fish and waterfowl. Ten species of wildfowl and waders overwinter in internationally important numbers on the Thames estuary.
>
> **Tidal creeks**
>
> These are found at the mouths of tributary rivers and streams. They act as important refuge areas for fish and are important feeding areas for birds such as grey heron and cormorant.
>
> **Salt marsh**
>
> This develops from continued deposition and colonisation of mudflats by plants. The largest remaining areas along the Thames are located on the north-east coast of Canvey Island, the south-east coast of Two Tree Island, and at Holehaven Creek. Upper salt marsh supports the most diverse range of flora and invertebrates, adapted to survive in saline conditions. Nationally scarce plants found on adapted Thames salt marsh include: golden samphire, Borrer's saltmarsh grass, and two nationally scarce species of eelgrass. Salt marsh is also an important habitat for breeding or roosting waterfowl and is important in providing a natural form of flood defence.
>
> **Grazing marsh**
>
> Grazing marsh has been created over centuries by enclosure of salt marsh by sea walls. It is distinctive owing to its brackish influence

which supports nationally scarce plants and invertebrates. The reasons for this brackishness are unclear. Factors include retention of salt from the former salt marshes, small catchment sizes and low rainfall. There is also some seepage of seawater through the sluices in the sea wall.

The juxtaposition of grazing marshes with the extensive salt marshes and mudflats allows them to support internationally important bird populations. Wading birds often roost on the grazing marsh when pushed off the mudflats by the rising tide. The grazing marshes also support raptors such as marsh harrier and short-eared owl, which require extensive hunting ranges, and are also very important for breeding waterfowl such as lapwing and redshank.

(Adapted from Thames Estuary Partnership, 1999, p. 24)

SAQ 3.10   The impact of tidal defences on wildlife in the Thames estuary

Outline how, according to Box 3.3, the building of tidal defences has affected the habitats and species found in the Thames estuary.

3.3.2   A bird's eye view

As pointed out in Part 1, it can be difficult to define the boundaries of a city. Should they surround the physical buildings or its area of influence, its hinterland? Should they surround the town centre only or its suburbs, the places where its inhabitants work or where they live? The answer to each of these questions would produce different physical boundaries, sometimes markedly different in what they include. While they can be a convenient shorthand to describe a city, they also leave out a lot. This is because of the open nature of cities. People and goods and invisible communications, including financial transactions, are continuously moving in and out of cities and contributing to their growth and development, often ignoring any notional boundary. The only boundaries even noticed by plants and animals are those that coincide with physical barriers, walls or rivers for example, and these are as likely to be viewed as new habitats as they are barriers. This is how Reichholf, quoted earlier, describes how the capital city of Germany might appear to a bird flying above it:

If we [take an aerial view] of a city, let's say Berlin, [...] we see a combination of [open] land covered with buildings, more or less forest-like structures (parks and real forests) but also lakes and rivers with a multitude of other small-scale habitats contained in it. [...]

[...] If we take a closer look at the structure of cities we will find a structural richness in general. Moreover, this structural richness of buildings and open spaces is combined with green areas with low levels of nutrient input. Though from the utilisation point of view they appear rather inappropriate these conditions are very favourable to the development of urban biodiversity. [...]

But within the cities of Central Europe there are not only species that are common and widespread and thus of less interest for the protection of species; rather you can find very well some of the so called flagship species within those cities. The Peregrine Falcon, for example, considered as a particularly endangered species some decades ago, [now has found its] safest breeding area within cities. No climbers will disturb the broods at the Cologne Cathedral or at other churches […], as well as at the towers of power and heat supply stations. As breeding areas these places are safer than anywhere else in the countryside. This holds true for Eagle Owls and many other bird species.

(Reichholf, 2008)

Many other features of cities contribute to their attraction or otherwise for species. The urban heat island is just one example: large cities are often warmer, particularly at night, and have become popular night resting places for certain birds such as starlings that spend the night together in large colonies.

Like many other cities, London's urban habitats now support several rare bird species. The Corporation of London (the organisation responsible for the centre of London that made up much of the seventeenth century city and is now home to one of the city's main business and financial centres) produced a *Biodiversity Action Plan* in 2002. It identified three habitats and three threatened bird species to be monitored as an indication of local biodiversity. The three habitats it identified are city gardens, vertical habitats – the walls, balconies, terraces and roofs of tall buildings – and the Thames foreshore. The three bird species are the black redstart, peregrine falcon and house sparrow (see Figures 3.13 and 3.14). The Corporation's action plan aims to promote the importance of these birds and improve their habitats, where possible, to encourage their population (Corporation of London, 2002).

London is the most important site for the black redstart, a bird that has fewer than 100 pairs nesting in Britain, where it is rarer than the osprey. According to the Corporation of London, the population in the capital makes up between 10% and 30% of the national breeding population. It is a robin-sized member of the thrush family that occupies rooftops of derelict buildings and did particularly well in the ruined buildings found after the Second World War (Corporation of London, 2002).

A more dramatic recent coloniser of cities in the UK is the peregrine falcon (Figure 3.14), the fastest bird in the world. This raptor, which now thrives on urban pigeons, was actively destroyed in the Second World War because it attacked carrier pigeons used to carry messages. Then, like many top predators, it declined markedly as a result of poisoning from the persistent pesticide DDT. Now numbers have increased again and there are about 1400 breeding pairs in the UK, of which 60 live in cities including London, Brighton, Cardiff, Liverpool, Exeter and Portsmouth. Cities provide many examples of their preferred habitat: high places with lack of local disturbance and good food supply, and peregrine falcons are adapting to city life. According to the Royal Society for the Protection of Birds (Dixon and Shawyer, n.d.), peregrines usually eat other birds, mostly pigeons, but they have been known to dine on birds ranging in size from the tiny

Figure 3.13 Indicator species: (a) black redstart; (b) male house sparrow; (c) female house sparrow

Figure 3.14 A peregrine falcon feeding its chicks

goldcrest to the large grey heron. They also occasionally eat mammals, amphibians and large insects.

Peregrines have been particularly attracted to some of London's taller and more prestigious landmarks. The first breeding pair settled in Battersea's disused power station in 2000 then others moved to some prime sites, high buildings near the city centre: Tate Modern, the Barbican Centre and a penthouse overlooking Regent's Park where there was a plentiful supply of their main food, the London pigeon. (Corporation of London, 2002)

SAQ 3.11   How the urban environment supports peregrine falcons

Make notes on the aspects of urban environments that have led to the rise of the peregrine falcon in European cities. Use the headings: Habitats, Food, Protection and Other.

3.3.3   The case of the vanishing sparrow

Today the bird that is most associated with London by locals and visitors alike is the pigeon, an extraordinarily successful general scavenger that has resisted campaigns to remove it from public spaces. To earlier generations, two other birds symbolised London: the nightingale and the sparrow. The nightingale disappeared a long time ago from London, and is mostly celebrated by the sentimental song 'A nightingale sang in Berkeley Square', though it could well thrive again in modern London. Much more puzzling, however, has been the sharp decline of the house sparrow in many towns and cities, particularly in London, where it was so common that it was known as the 'cockney' sparrow. This has led to an intense discussion as to the reason or reasons for its decline, which are worthy of a good detective story.

A common feature of many urban environments is that they are often changing rapidly and this creates continual challenges and opportunities for urban organisms. For this reason, 'the most unnatural landscapes on the planet' quoted in the previous section can also serve as a modern laboratory to study the complex responses of species, ecosystems and habitats to rapid change. If Darwin were alive today he might well be studying house sparrows in London rather than finches in the Galapagos! This is how the City of London Biodiversity Action Plan describes the situation:

> Once among the most common birds in Britain, the Sparrow is now giving conservationists a real cause for concern. There are currently between six and seven million pairs of Sparrow in Britain, compared to just over twelve million pairs in the 1970s. The problem is particularly evident in London where

numbers have fallen by 59% between 1994 and 2000. Current research is being carried out by the British Trust for Ornithology and the Royal Society for the Protection of Birds (RSPB) to identify the reasons for this decline. Reasons put forward include:

- lack of food for chicks e.g. aphids and other insects
- reduction of nest sites through renovation of old buildings
- effect of predation by crows, magpies, grey squirrels and cats
- changes in agriculture
- the impact of lead free petrol on aphids (reducing numbers)
- removal of 'weeds' such as Docks and Chickweed that Sparrows like to eat.

(Corporation of London, 2002)

Part of its action plan is to undertake a survey of sparrow numbers in open spaces that it owns or manages, and it is reviewing pesticide use in city open spaces. However, in order to protect the sparrow, people must first identify the real reasons why it appears to be vanishing. Plenty of ideas have been put forward, but until there is some evidence to show what is really happening, progress may be limited. In May 2000, *The Independent* newspaper started a campaign, Save The Sparrow, by offering a £5000 prize for a convincing theory. Eight-and-a-half years later they thought they might have found the answer. What do you think? Read the article 'Mystery of the vanishing sparrow' from *The Independent* then answer SAQ 3.12.

Mystery of the vanishing sparrow

The Independent offered £5,000 for a convincing theory about why the house sparrow was dying out in cities. The answer seems to lie with falling insect numbers, reports Michael McCarthy

Michael McCarthy

The Independent, 20 November 2008

It's taken eight-and-a-half years – but *The Independent's* £5,000 prize for explaining the disappearance of the house sparrow from our towns and cities finally has a serious entry, with a serious theory.

Insect decline, featured prominently in this newspaper last Saturday, is offered as the reason for the biggest bird mystery of modern times by a group of four scientists from the Royal Society for the Protection of Birds (RSPB), De Montfort University in Leicester and Natural England, the Government's wildlife agency.

Their theory, put forward in a scientific paper to be published in a forthcoming issue of the journal Animal Conservation, is based on intensive research in Leicester, showing that sparrow chicks were starving in their nests because their parents could not find enough insects to feed them. So many chicks were dying that the birds' population level as a whole was declining.

The paper has been entered for *The Independent's* prize, which was reported around the world when it was announced on 16 May 2000, as the start of a campaign to Save The Sparrow.

One of the authors, Dr Kate Vincent, who carried out the research on which the theory is based, said: 'If we were successful, given the statuses of the collaborating organisations, we feel that any prize money received should be spent on further research or conservation work on house sparrows. From *The Independent's* point of view it would be a natural progression to know that your Save The Sparrow campaign prize money would be engineering further sparrow research, which we feel would be something to celebrate.'

The £5,000 prize was offered for a peer-reviewed paper published in a scientific journal, which – in the opinion of our referees – would account for the disappearance of the house sparrow, Passer domesticus, from towns and cities in Britain. The referees are the RSPB, the British Trust for Ornithology (BTO), and Dr Denis Summers-Smith, an internationally renowned expert on sparrows. (It was stated at the time that researchers from the RSPB and BTO would not be precluded from entering.) The referees will now be considering the paper to see if it does indeed account for a remarkable wildlife enigma.

House sparrows in Britain have declined by 68 per cent since 1977, but the decline has been overwhelmingly an urban one. Although still relatively plentiful in small towns in the countryside and by the sea, in many major conurbations, sparrows have disappeared. Numbers started falling in cities in the mid-1980s and the species has virtually vanished from central London – for example, St James's Park holds all the common garden birds such as blue tits, robins and blackbirds, but sparrows, which were once plentiful, died out in the park in the late 1990s. There was no obvious cause. House sparrows are also disappearing from Bristol, Edinburgh and Dublin, as well as Hamburg, Prague and Moscow but curiously, they are faring better in Paris and Berlin.

When *The Independent* launched its campaign, many potential reasons for the decline were suggested by readers, which included increased predation by cats, magpies and sparrowhawks (all of which have increased in our cities); disease contracted from bird food such as peanuts; increased use of pesticides; collective suicide; radiation from the Chernobyl nuclear accident in the former USSR; the disappearance of sparrow nesting places as houses were modernised and gardens were tidied up or concreted over as car ports, and a decline in insects. (Although adult sparrows are seed-eating birds, the young need insect food in the first few days of their lives).

The last two potential causes – lack of nesting places and insect shortage – have always seemed the most likely (although many people blame magpies and other predators for declines in small birds, both the RSPB and the BTO say this is not borne out by the figures).

A leading proponent of the insect shortage theory was Dr Summers-Smith, a retired engineer from Guisborough in Cleveland, and the author of the standard monograph on the house sparrow, and several other sparrow books. He felt that chick starvation might well be the cause of the fall in numbers as a whole, although he was unable to prove it.

This appears to have been borne out in the new paper. The lead author, Dr Will Peach from the RSPB, said: 'Each pair of house sparrows must rear at least five chicks every year to stop their numbers falling.

'But in our study, too many chicks were starving in their nests. Others were fledging [leaving the nest] but were too weak to live for much longer than that. If the birds nested in areas rich in insects, they did much better.

'Where there were few insects, young house sparrows were likely to die. Young house sparrows need insects rather than seeds, peanuts or bread to survive.'

Dr Vincent, then of De Montfort University in Leicester, said: 'This is one of the most mysterious and complex declines of a species in recent years. The study highlights that sparrow chicks are hatching but they aren't surviving.

'This is partly down to the loss of green spaces within British cities through development on green space, tree removal and the conversion of front gardens for parking. The loss of deciduous greenery within urban areas may have made life much more difficult for birds like house sparrows that need large numbers of insects to feed their young.'

Phil Grice, senior ornithologist at Natural England, said: 'This study highlights the importance of using native varieties of plants in our urban green spaces which, in turn, support large numbers of insects that are important in the diet of house sparrows and a range of other birds that we love to see in our gardens'.

The paper, Reproductive success of house sparrows along an urban gradient, by W J Peach, K E Vincent, J A Fowler and P V Grice, is now being sent to our referees and we shall report soon on their verdict.

SAQ 3.12   The mystery of the vanishing sparrow

Answer the following questions, based on your reading of 'Mystery of the vanishing sparrow'.

1   List the ideas put forward to account for the vanishing sparrow and try to place them under the headings of Changing habitat, Food, Predators and Other.

2   Describe briefly the evidence to support the idea that lack of insects is a major cause.

3   One of the comments accompanying the article suggested microwave radiation from mobile telephone masts as the cause: 'Our bird numbers have dropped alarmingly and bees are almost non-existent. Also moths and butterflies.' Can you think of evidence from the article that would counter this?

For wildlife and biodiversity more generally, there are winners and losers in the adaptation race to occupy the urban environment. Urban environments are rich in unusual habitats, in resources such as food waste, which provides opportunities for some species, but is harmful to others. Animals and plants that can take advantage of this unnatural abundance, such as general scavengers: some birds, arthropods, introduced and exotic plants in parks and gardens, can thrive.

The real winners may be a very few 'urban adapted' species, the generalist scavengers, that have learnt to live in close proximity with humans (whether we want them to or not) and are found in cities around the world: cockroaches, rats, pigeons, foxes and, particularly in the developed world, domestic pets.

Summary of Section 3

Cities have to adapt to avoid becoming vulnerable to the growing threats posed by global environmental change. Section 3 looked at two examples of the threats posed by climate change, heatwaves and flooding, and explored positive ways in which cities can adapt to environmental change and reduce their vulnerability, taking London as an example.

Plants and animals are continuously adapting to their environments and cities offer them new environments and a variety of new habitats. Some surprising species are adapting to special niches in cities, others are threatened by the changes and declining, while certain generalist species thrive in proximity to human communities and urban environments.

Creative people, creative solutions

4

Cities and their populations are the major cause of environmental changes throughout the world, either directly from their local impacts or indirectly through the global economic and political power of their institutions, their demands for food and other resources, and the wastes and emissions produced. They are also vulnerable to environmental change. Block 6 has explored how cities, using the example of London, have responded to threats and disasters caused by environmental change, and are now attempting to reduce both their environmental impacts and their vulnerability to future change by adaptation. Its focus has been on finding positive solutions to problems on all scales from local, city-wide to global.

Global environmental problems can often seem overwhelming in their scale, and the threats they pose in many parts of the world, as this course has shown on its journey, cannot be ignored. In the face of global climate change and massive loss to biodiversity the actions of individuals or local groups can seem almost irrelevant, but everywhere that the course has visited you have encountered people who are trying to understand what is happening in their localities and to their communities and finding solutions. In this section I hope to follow their positive examples of 'thinking globally, acting locally' by showing how creative ideas and actions from groups and individuals can play an active role in shaping the development of their community, this time using the example of a small city in Germany.

Before turning to this example, I would like to remind you of a framework for categorising the institutions that influence our daily life. The idea of the 'interlocking spheres' of the state, the market and civil society was introduced at the beginning of the course, in Part 4 of Block 1. The state makes the laws and regulations and enforces them, the markets represent businesses and private enterprise, and civil society is made up of a variety of voluntary organisations or groupings of people. The key point made about this framework is that in most situations all three of these connected spheres should be engaged to achieve sustainable action in a democratic society. For example, Section 2 of Part 3 discussed the potential of eco-cities to provide a model for sustainable urban living in the future, but a criticism of this approach is that these cities are being planned and created top down and not with the engagement of the people who will live in them. State and market are coming together, but civil society has yet to be involved. Involving and engaging people voluntarily in any large-scale project can be difficult, as examples in this block from London have shown. Keep in mind the roles of state, market and civil society as you read through this final example of a city and one of its neighbourhoods that has attempted to become more sustainable with the broad support of its people.

The city in question is Freiburg in southern Germany, a city of approximately 200 000 people situated at the edge of the broad valley of the River Rhine. It is close to the mountains of the Black Forest and occupies one of the sunniest locations in Germany. Freiburg is sometimes called Germany's 'Solar City' (see Box 3.4).

Box 3.4   The evolution of a Solar City

Freiburg has many claims to be a green city, not least because it has been working towards this end for more than 40 years. Like many German cities, Freiburg had to be rebuilt after 1945, which was done by widening existing streets to make space for a network of trams. In the 1970s, regional authorities planned to build a nuclear power plant just outside Freiburg. This led to protest and civil disobedience and the plans were defeated in 1975. However, Freiburg then decided to act positively and find other 'green' ways of meeting its energy requirements. The old town centre had recently become pedestrian and a low speed limit (30 kph) was set for most of the town, while plans were laid for cycle paths and lanes to be established. A wide network of environmental organisations, businesses and research institutes were also founded and in 1986, shortly after the nuclear disaster at Chernobyl, Freiburg's municipal council voted to adopt the guidelines for an energy policy based on energy conservation, the use of new technologies such as combined heat and power, and the use of renewable energy sources such as solar to meet new demand, instead of fossil fuels. This is the same 'lean, green, clean' model now adopted by London's Climate Change Action Plan. In 1996 it adopted a resolution to cut the city's 1992 carbon dioxide emissions by a quarter by 2010.

It has made considerable progress towards becoming a 'Green City' in some sectors:

Recycling: annual waste has been reduced from 140 000 tonnes in 1986 to 50 000 tonnes by 2000.

Travel: most journeys in the urban region are by foot, bicycle or public transport and two-thirds of the population live within walking distance of a tram stop. Five hundred kilometres of cycle paths have been created.

However, Freiburg has made its name as the solar city. There are over a thousand (photovoltaic) solar installations ranging from individual houses to football stadiums, schools and swimming pools, as well as passive solar heaters (Figure 3.15). These solar panels feed electricity into the local grid and are paid a premium rate for it. This guaranteed tariff was established by government legislation and applies across Germany. In addition, the main regional power supplier, Bodeva (which was set up by regional councils) subsidises the installation of solar panels. There is now more installed capacity in this region than in the whole of the UK.

Freiburg has created successful businesses designing, building and promoting green energy. Ten thousand people work in 1500 organisations in the environmental and solar industries, including 700 in solar technology. These include a major solar energy research institute, a solar factory and a variety of public and private agencies, consultancies, agricultural cooperatives and workshops. Its role as an international showcase for solar energy attracts people and organisations from around the world; there is even a zero-emission hotel to stay in. But it also pays considerable attention to environmental education and activities in schools and to

(a)

(c)

(b)

(d)

Figure 3.15 Solar panels in Freiburg: (a) residential complex; (b) Badenova stadium; (c) Vauban solar village; (d) Vauban tram line

citizen participation and engagement in its future plans for the city region.

The sustainable model district of Vauban is a showcase for many visitors. This is a new development to the south of the city of about 6000 people living in 2000 dwellings, built on the site of an old French Barracks. The project was begun in 1993

> to implement a city district in a co-operative, participatory way which meets ecological, social, economical and cultural requirements
>
> *(Vauban, n.d.)*

Participation played a key part and the citizens' association, an NGO, was given legal rights by the city to coordinate it. For example:

> The streets and public spaces at Vauban have been carefully planned. They are playgrounds for children and places for social interaction. The design of the public green spaces, streets and the neighbourhood centre at Vauban were developed during meetings and workshops with residents.
>
> *(Commission for Architecture and the Built Environment, n.d.)*

The character of the district has been created by banning both detached houses and buildings more than four stories high, leading to compact urban structures, but diversity has been encouraged by allocating land in small plots to private builders and cooperatives. Houses are built to the highest ecological standards, many with solar panels, and at least a hundred dwellings produce more energy than they need and sell it to the grid. The residents are mainly well-off families with young children, but include students living in accommodation and 10% of social housing. Residential areas that are car free, with green spaces and corridors, surround a centre that has bus and tram connections to the city. Over half of the residents do not have cars, but have access to car-sharing schemes. Cars are parked on the periphery of the area or in a large, solar-powered community car park.

> A district centre has been created at Vauban with shops, a primary school, kindergartens and public green spaces.

Vauban has been designed to create a 'district of short distances' where the schools, farmer's market, businesses, shopping centre, food coop, recreation areas and approximately 600 jobs will be within walking and cycling distance of residents.

(Commission for Architecture and the Built Environment, n.d.)

The majority of those who have bought houses in Vauban still live there, and enjoy their houses and way of life. It would seem to be an ideal environment for bringing up young children but some parents are worried that it may be less appealing to teenagers. There have also been a few rumblings of discontent, clashes even, between those wishing to use cars and those who want to ban them completely. The houses are also not cheap, so the district is sometimes viewed by other districts as a trendy middle-class enclave, i.e. not really diverse or representative of the whole city.

The Freiburg Solar City project is a continuing one. It has been highly successful in promoting new environmental technologies and providing employment in these areas. It has also created in Vauban an urban district that continues on its path towards sustainability, by taking care to involve its communities. There is one area, however, where there has been less success than hoped, and that is in reducing the carbon footprint of the city. It was reduced by only 5% between 1993 and 2003 and will fail in its target to cut it by 25% in 2010, although it has ambitious plans for the future. This is largely explained by its earlier reliance on nuclear power for electricity generation, a low-carbon source, which it has cut from 60% to 30%. The majority now comes from combined heat and power plants, which are efficient but do not use renewable energy. Surprisingly, only 4% is contributed by renewable energy: 2% from local solar sources and 2% from wind farms on nearby hills (as in the UK there has been opposition to further development), though the city plans to increase the proportion from renewables to 10%. This one figure perhaps encapsulates the difficulties of developing new environmental technologies and moving towards a lower carbon footprint.

SAQ 3.13   The role of state, markets and civil society

Box 3.4 described the evolution of Freiburg towards a solar city. Give an example of how the three 'interlocking spheres' of state, markets and civil society worked together.

This example illustrates how people, collectively, can make significant changes to the way they live. It also shows that on the key measure of carbon footprints, which serves as a good proxy for environmental impacts generally, there is still a long, long way to go. Most scientists agree that to avoid dangerous climate change (a global mean temperature rise of more than 2 °C), the carbon footprints of developed countries will need to be cut by up to 90%, and that the cuts need to start as soon as possible. This is going to be a tremendous challenge, because even the examples from Masdar and Dongtan did not claim to be able to reduce their footprints by 90%, though this was the eventual aim. The discussion at the beginning of the course, which used the device of carbon 'wedges' to illustrate how it would be possible to reduce global emissions by making changes to major industries and patterns of consumption, has been overtaken by events and we would have to add a lot more 'wedges' now.

The good news is that initiatives such as those from Freiburg and Vauban are being replicated in thousands of villages, towns and cities around the world. The C40 group and the initiatives associated with them, mentioned in Part 2, is one example. Another, more grass-roots approach which illustrates the actions of civil society is the transition network movement (TransitionNetwork, n.d.) that has been growing rapidly in several countries including the UK. Many countries, including the UK, have committed to reducing their carbon footprints significantly by 2050, but have yet to provide the means of doing so, while international negotiations seem to drag on, making little progress, not helped by the reluctance until recently of the USA to play a major role. This lack of real progress from nation states has even led major multinational companies to start lobbying for more effective action and to create 'level playing fields' so that they can take action on the environment without losing out in competition with those who would avoid it.

And if we don't act, what then? Over the first decade of this century, the rate at which we have been adding greenhouse gases to the atmosphere is the highest ever, and they are accumulating in the atmosphere much faster than expected. The trend has recently been exceeding even the 'worst-case scenario' for emissions, which has now become more likely. The following is a recent press report from the Meteorological Office's Hadley Centre on what this will lead to.

> If greenhouse gas emissions continue to rise unchecked, it is likely that global warming will exceed four degrees by the end of the century, research by Met Office scientists has revealed.

181

If current high emissions continue there could be major implications for the world – with higher temperature rises than previously thought.

Dr Richard Betts, Head of Climate Impacts at the Met Office Hadley Centre, presented the new findings, *4 degrees and beyond*, which is the first to consider the global consequences of climate change beyond 2 °C.

Dr Betts said: 'Four degrees of warming, averaged over the globe, translates into even greater warming in many regions, along with major changes in rainfall. If greenhouse gas emissions are not cut soon, we could see major climate changes within our own lifetimes.'

In some areas warming could be significantly higher (10 degrees or more).

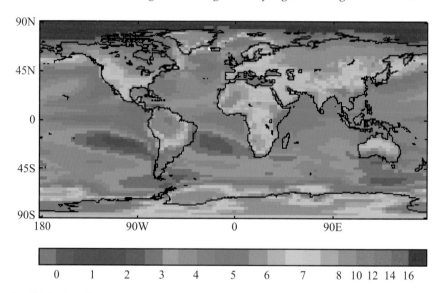

[… Global surface] temperature increases between 1961–1990 and 2090–2099 [for the 'four degrees and beyond' scenario]

The Arctic could warm by up to 15 °C for a high-emissions scenario, enhanced by melting of snow and ice causing more of the Sun's radiation to be absorbed.

For Africa, the western and southern regions are expected to experience both large warming (up to 10 °C) and drying.

[Many] land areas could warm by seven degrees or more.

Rainfall could decrease by 20% or more in some areas, although there is a spread in the magnitude of drying. All computer models indicate reductions in rainfall over western and southern Africa, Central America, the Mediterranean and parts of coastal Australia.

In other areas, such as India, rainfall could increase by 20% or more. Higher rainfall increases the risk of river flooding.

Dr Betts added: 'Together these impacts will have very large consequences for food security, water availability and health. However, it is possible to avoid these dangerous levels of temperature rise by cutting greenhouse gas emissions. If global emissions peak within the next decade and then decrease rapidly it may be possible to avoid at least half of the four degrees of warming.'

(Meteorological Office, 2009)

Ultimately our future is in our own hands. If we are to avoid for our children's sake, if not our own, the scary scenario outlined above we are going to have to make major changes to our lifestyles – or it will be 'done' to us by environmental disasters and collapsing ecosystem services. That means not just making the easy decisions where most people gain, but also difficult decisions where sacrifices have to be made. It depends ultimately on what we all think and believe can and should be done. In other words, the views and opinions of individuals matter.

At the start of the course, in Block 1, you carried out two activities: Activity 1.1 asked you for your opinions about the environment, and Activity 4.2 for your views about the future. Were you pessimistic or optimistic? Who should be responsible for taking action: individuals, communities, businesses or government? Have your own views changed over the eight months between the start and the end of the course? If so, how?

You will be prompted to think about this as you embark on your final assignment, but you will also have the opportunity to compare notes on your experience, if you wish, with a wider community and to contribute to a project where people's opinions on the environment are tracked for a decade. For the assignment itself you have an opportunity to put forward your own proposal to solve an environmental problem.

Before finishing this section and to end on a positive note, I recommend you listen to 'Wind power: a personal journey' on the course DVD, presented by a member of the course team.

Summary of Section 4

This section looked at the story of Freiburg's moves to become a 'solar city', emphasising the roles played by state, markets and civil society, and the importance of engaging people at individual, community and institutional levels to effect positive change for any environmental initiative.

5   Journey's end?

You have now reached the end of *Environment: journeys through a changing world*, which has taken you on two learning journeys. The first has been a journey to key regions of the planet to learn about the local impacts of global environmental change from the experiences of those living and working there. You have been exposed to different approaches to understanding the complexities of environmental issues and to *debates* and discussion about what to do – who and what is important and should be protected, what kind of world we want. You have explored some of the *processes* that maintain our living world, the many flows and connections – physical, biological and ecological, social – that also contribute to environmental change. You have also examined the *strategies* of different groups as they attempt to respond to and manage environmental problems using a variety of styles, techniques and approaches and involving different groups of stakeholders.

The second journey has been the development of your own, personal knowledge and skills. The course has provided both generic study skills and exposure to some methods and techniques of study from different disciplines. Each of you will have approached these aids to study in your own way, depending on your own needs and interests, background and experience. If, having studied this course, you feel that you are now more informed about environmental issues and more aware of their complexities and possible solutions, then your time has been well spent.

However, if there is *one message* to take away from studying an interdisciplinary course I hope it is this: whatever your own views and perceptions, we all have to listen to and understand the views and perceptions of others. Doing this allows us to have fruitful discussions and enriches our understanding. It does not mean that we never have to make up our mind or make choices; it does mean that we are more informed when making them.

The four course aims are listed in the *Course Guide*. This is an appropriate moment to read them once more. They are to:

- help you understand the current debates regarding our environment and sustainability and enable you to participate from an informed position
- show how the planet undergoes a process of environmental change brought about by human activity and natural processes
- recognise and engage with strategies that might counter the adverse effects of human activity on our environment
- prepare you for further academic study by helping you to develop your study skills.

The course team hopes that you have been stimulated to study more about the environment, particularly if this is your first major university course. There are a range of courses available that will allow you to follow pathways in environment and many other areas. If you have enjoyed the debates then you may wish to investigate the Social Sciences. An interest in the processes may suggest the Sciences and an engagement with strategies and solutions a look at Technology. There are also further interdisciplinary courses in Environment, Development Studies and related areas.

Studying this course opens up many choices to you for further study. So this is not the end of the journey but part of a continuing journey, perhaps with the suggestion of some new directions. It may also have led you to think more about the everyday choices you make for yourself and with your family. We live in an interconnected world where our personal choices and those of others affect everyone and every living being.

I would like to end with a poem by Robert Frost, an American poet who celebrated the world about him. This poem is about journeys and choices, appropriate topics for learning and life, but like many poems is open to different interpretations. What it says to me is that there are times in life when we have to make choices, difficult choices possibly, and then we live with the consequences, foreseen and unforeseen. To avoid doing this is to learn nothing and not really living. Choose wisely!

The road not taken

Robert Frost

Mountain Interval, 1916

Two roads diverged in a yellow wood,
And sorry I could not travel both
And be one traveler, long I stood
And looked down one as far as I could
To where it bent in the undergrowth;

Then took the other, as just as fair
And having perhaps the better claim,
Because it was grassy and wanted wear;
Though as for that, the passing there
Had worn them really about the same,

And both that morning equally lay
In leaves no step had trodden black
Oh, I kept the first for another day!
Yet knowing how way leads on to way,
I doubted if I should ever come back.

I shall be telling this with a sigh
somewhere ages and ages hence:
two roads diverged in a wood, and I –
I took the one less traveled by,
And that has made all the difference.

Summary of Part 3

Cities have historically served economic, social and sometimes political purposes. Part 3 asked what a city would be like if environmental concerns were added to this list, to re-imagine the city as an ecological entity. The economic, social and environmental aspects of two possible approaches were explored: building an eco-city from scratch and greening the spaces of existing cities. However they develop in the future, the cities of today have to adapt to environmental changes to avoid suffering damage. Introducing 'green' ideas can help, but so also can simple changes in social organisation and preparedness. The future of the planet is grim unless we can all change our lifestyles. Part of the solution may lie in actions at a local level exemplified by those from Freiburg.

After completing Part 3 you should be able to:

- identify the relative importance of economic, social and environmental factors in supporting sustainable actions

- discuss ecological principles in urban design

- explore and assess positive ways that cities can adapt to environmental change and reduce their vulnerability

- appreciate the need to engage people at individual, community and institutional levels to effect positive change

- read and use articles written from a range of points of view and for a range of audiences.

Answers to SAQs

SAQ 3.1

1   The economic and environmental costs of using large numbers of horses inside a city seem to be high. The 50 000 horses used for trams and buses needed a quarter of a million acres of foodstuff per year, and deposited 1000 tonnes of dung on the roads every day, which then had to be disposed of. This was costly economically (keeping horses accounted for more than half of operating costs) and dung on the streets was a major nuisance and pollutant. The change to electric trams removed a major pollution problem, but it also changed employment. Trams, running on tracks, also had disadvantages: tracks were expensive to maintain and trams could only go where there were tracks. Buses had greater flexibility of routes and were more comfortable to use.

2   For Londoners the changes brought many advantages and some disadvantages, and no doubt some groups benefited more than others. With the disappearance of horse transport, Londoners could walk and ride on cleaner streets and poor areas no longer had to put up with the disposal of dung. More mobility and greater comfort helped commuting and development of suburbs. The livelihoods and skills required of many working in transport changed as horses were replaced by mechanisation, although we are not told whether employment increased or decreased. Death and injury from road traffic accidents rose considerably.

SAQ 3.2

1   The main principle is to keep cities compact, in order to reduce energy use. Register argues that to achieve this towns and cities should become more three-dimensional, like natural structures (he contrasts New York with the flat urban sprawl that characterises many towns in North America). However, he also argues for diversity in the built environment, for a mixture of high-density living (e.g. city flats), serviced by transport, side by side with low-density, greener spaces (e.g. parks and rivers).

He also mentions a variety of other suggestions: very efficient recycling, pedestrian and cycle paths, restoration of natural areas, more energy-efficient buildings, use of sunlight and green roofs, but emphasises that compactness is the key.

2   The most notable feature of early towns or cities is that they were compact. This meant that inhabitants could get most of what they wanted by walking; there were few alternatives. Because cheap energy was not available they were not based on a high-energy infrastructure, using instead systems like waterways (e.g. Venice) for transport. (The old centres of many modern towns still show this feature, what Register calls the logic of access by proximity, and many today have been returned to mainly pedestrian use.)

SAQ 3.3

1   Use of compactness in the design of the cities. Both cities are designed to be compact; in Dongtan, for example, no one will be more than seven minutes' walk from public transport and only electric vehicles are allowed in the city areas. This feature is also part of the design that both use to reduce energy use. In addition, both source energy by renewable means and recycle materials as much as possible. Only Masdar could be said to be three-dimensional with its use of conical wind towers to provide lighting and cooling and its two-tier structure of a pedestrian deck, separated from traffic, above an underground space for a podcar network.

2   Encouraging diversity can mean diversity of its populations, the built environment, and biodiversity. The articles say very little about the mix of inhabitants, although Wood argues that Dongtan is designed for a mixed community. Both plan a mix of fairly dense buildings and spaces. Dongtan encourages a range of innovative designs, while housing in Masdar seems more uniform. Both are surrounded by green buffer zones, for wildlife in Dongtan's case, and to provide 'green lungs' for Masdar.

3   Dongtan aims to reduce energy consumption by two-thirds, and to use renewables and waste as energy sources, including a CHP plant based on burning rice husks from elsewhere (so will have an additional footprint). It plans to reduce waste sent to landfill to zero eventually. Masdar plans to reduce its energy use by 80% using passive methods of cooling, and use renewables (solar panels and wind farms) for energy and desalination. It is not clear whether it is truly zero-carbon or not. It also plans to reduce water use by a similar amount through conservation and recycling, and to reduce biological waste to zero.

SAQ 3.4

1   Both use teams of British architects. The Dongtan project has commissioned Arup. The global engineering consultancy is mentioned, in partnership with the Shanghai Industrial Investment Company, which is not mentioned. Masdar is employing Foster and Partners.

2   Both cities pay attention to the local climate, which has a major bearing on their design. In Masdar, keeping cool and preserving water are key considerations, which is the reason for the orientation of the city and the narrow passageways in place of roads, and features such as drought-resistant green spaces. In Dongtan, where there is a warm, humid climate, the surrounding habitats are the main restraint, but also a design influence. The city is more open to the surroundings, houses need little insulation and agricultural materials are used as fuel. Both also reflect the cultures of their local populations in their housing and street designs.

SAQ 3.5

The basic argument for building new eco-cities is that they provide living laboratories for testing green ideas and principles.

Dongtan is unproven and eco-cities – starting from scratch – are a luxury. Realistically, to build for the population of the future involves working with what is already there and working with existing communities who can say what they want. This means changing existing cities or 'retrofitting'. What has changed recently is the realisation that large-scale retrofitting, of a whole street for example, is feasible.

SAQ 3.6

A sustainable initiative should be able to demonstrate that it provides environmental, social and economic benefits, in other words a 'win-win-win' situation. The environmental benefits are spelt out in the GLA excerpt and Box 3.1. They include pollution reduction, support for biodiversity and climate modification (protection from floods and heat). The social benefits are described in the excerpt from the Department of Communities and Local Government and, as Activity 3.2 points out, provide physical, social and psychological benefits. The economic benefits, such as urban regeneration and employment, are less clear cut, but broadly speaking green spaces provide their services free so that the cost to society is mostly that of maintaining the green spaces in good condition. This would appear to be good value.

SAQ 3.7

1   Most air conditioners send hot air into the streets outside buildings, adding to the direct heat effect. They also add to local or regional pollution from the fossil fuels burned to power them unless they use renewable power. Both effects worsen the immediate impacts of a heatwave for others. They also contribute to the greenhouse gas burden, thus increasing the chances of more heatwaves in the future.

2   Green spaces and urban trees can help to reduce the urban heat island as well as providing cool spaces during hot weather. Urban design could be used to adapt existing buildings (and streets) to provide more shade and insulation from heat.

3   Factors to consider for the longer term: designing buildings and streets to be suitable for warmer climates, taking measures to reduce the UHI and air pollution, and above all taking measures to reduce the carbon footprint and hence climate change.

SAQ 3.8

1   Flooding from the sea will increase as global sea levels rise. Changes to storm patterns may also increase the risk from tidal surges.

River flooding can be affected by deforestation of uplands and building on flood plains. Both add to the risk of flooding, and building near rivers increases the number of people likely to be affected. Climate change is also likely to increase flooding from heavier rainfall in winter and heavier *intensity* of rainfall in summer.

Surface run-off: it could be argued that this form of run-off is caused almost entirely by environmental changes, because without the built environment it would be far less common.

2   In urban areas green spaces of all types help to absorb rainfall and reduce flooding by surface run-off. Returning flood plains and wetlands to their original status improves the capacity of these areas to absorb flood waters and reduce their intensity.

SAQ 3.9

The Thames and its estuary provide a number of ecosystem services.

It supports many varieties of shipping and water transport and is a major artery for commerce and commodities.

The estuary and its mudflats provide habitats for a great variety of species including fish and birds.

It provides recreation on its waters and its banks are used by anglers, wildfowlers, cyclists, horse riders and bird watchers.

It has been used for centuries to flush away the waste of Londoners, but this role is being reduced.

SAQ 3.10

The construction of concrete embankments has led to the loss of some intertidal mudflats in the inner estuary, which would reduce the numbers of invertebrates, algae and eelgrass and the birds that feed on them.

Grazing marsh, in contrast, has been created by the enclosure by sea walls of salt marsh. They provide habitats for particular raptors and waterfowl. Their presence also increases the variety of habitats in the estuary and can provide roosts for wading birds.

SAQ 3.11

Habitats: tall buildings in cities provide the preferred habitat of peregrines, which is undisturbed high places.

Food: good food supply of pigeons and other birds.

Protection: now protected instead of being destroyed.

Other: banning of pesticide DDT.

SAQ 3.12

1   Reasons put forward for the decline of sparrows are:
    Changing habitat: lack of nesting places, loss of green spaces.
    Food: shortage of insects.
    Predators: increased predation from cats, magpies and sparrowhawks.
    Other: disease from bird food, collective suicide, radiation.

2   Research in Leicester showed that sparrow chicks were starving in the nests or dying soon after fledging because they were weakened because parents could not find enough insects. Birds nesting in areas rich in insects did better. They found that young sparrows need large numbers of insects to survive rather than other food.

3   House sparrows are mainly declining in large urban areas, but mobile telephone masts are found across the country.

SAQ 3.13

The history of Freiburg's move towards a 'solar city' illustrates this well. Initially a variety of organisations (civil society) objected to a nuclear plant and then lobbied successfully for their municipal council to adopt new energy policies. The use of solar energy was encouraged by government legislation (state) on the feed-in tariff, and supported by local industries (market) developing and using solar energy. The Bodeva power company is a hybrid between state and market.

References

Broxbourne (2008) *Green Corridors*, http://www.broxbourne.gov.uk/PDF/CS_13_ GreenCorridors_HD_FINAL.pdf (Accessed 15 October 2009).

Commission for Architecture and the Built Environment (n.d.), *Vauban, Freiburg Germany, Evaluation*, http://www.cabe.org.uk/case-studies/vauban/evaluation (Accessed 16 October 2009).

Corporation of London (2002) *Biodiversity Action Plan*, www.cityoflondon.gov.uk/bap (Accessed 14 October 2009).

Costello, A. et al. (2009) 'Managing the health effects of climate change', *The Lancet*, 16 May, p. 1693.

Department of Communities and Local Government (2009) *Communities and neighbourhoods: Parks and urban green spaces*, http://www.communities.gov.uk/ communities/sustainablecommunities/cleanersafergreener/parksurban/ (Accessed September 2009).

Department of Health (2009) *Heatwave Plan for England: protecting health and reducing harm from extreme heat and heatwaves*, revised edition, Crown copyright.

Dixon, N. and Shawyer, C. (n.d.) *Peregrine falcons: provision of artificial nest sites on built structures*, English Nature, RSPB and Corporation of London.

Elmqvist, T. E. (2008) *Expert input (Panel 1) to the Conference of Parties to the UN Conference on Biodiversity*, Bonn, Germany, May 2008, http://www.iclei.org/index. php?id=6834 (Accessed 15 October 2009).

Environment Agency (2009) The Thames Estuary: Thames Estuary Map, http://www. environment-agency.gov.uk/static/documents/Leisure/thamesestuarymap2_1674315.pdf (Accessed 1 December 2009).

Girardet, H. (1999) *Creating Sustainable Cities* (Schumacher Briefing No. 2), Totnes, Green Books, (reprinted version, 2007).

Global Public Media (2004) David Room interviewing Richard Register, 23 August, http://www.globalpublicmedia.com/transcripts/496 (Accessed August 2009).

Green Roof Consultancy (n.d.) 'Introduction to Green Roof Benefits', http://www. livingroofs.org/livingpages/greenroofbenefits.html (Accessed 14 October 2009).

Hadley Centre (2004) *Uncertainty, risk and dangerous climate change. Recent research on climate change science from the Hadley Centre*, December 2004, Meteorological Office and Department for Environment, Food and Rural Affairs.

Jenkins, G. J., Murphy, J. M., Sexton, D. M. H., Lowe, J. A., Jones, P. and Kilsby, C. G. (2009) *UK Climate Projections: Briefing report*, Exeter, Meteorological Office Hadley Centre.

Kovats, R., Johnson, H. and Griffiths, C. (2005) *Mortality in southern England during the 2003 heatwave by place of death*, Office for National Statistics.

London Transport Museum (2007) 'Travel revolution', http://www.ltmuseum.co.uk/tfl/ collections/guide/travel-revolution.aspx (Accessed 27 October 2009).

London Transport Museum (2008) 'Public transport in Victorian London. Part One: Overground', http://www.ltmcollection.org/resources/index.html?IXglossary=Public +transp ort+in+Victorian+London%3a+Part+One%3a+Overground (Accessed August 2009).

McCarthy, M. (2008) 'Mystery of the vanishing sparrow', *The Independent*, http://www. independent.co.uk/environment/nature/mystery-of-the-vanishing-sparrow-1026319.html (Accessed 6 October 2009).

Mayor of London (2006) *London's Urban Heat Island: A Summary for Decision Makers*, October, Greater London Authority.

Mayor of London (2008) *The London Climate Change Adaptation Strategy: Summary Draft Report*, August, Greater London Authority.

Meteorological Office (2009) 'Four degrees and beyond', http://www.metoffice.gov.uk/climatechange/news/latest/four-degrees.html (Accessed 16 October 2009).

Moore, R. (2009) 'Vertical gardens: the height of fashion', *London Evening Standard*, 18 May, http://www.thisislondon.co.uk/lifestyle/article-23693750-vertical-gardens-the-height-of-fashion.do (Accessed 14 October 2009).

Pool, R. (2009) 'A tale of two cities', *IET Knowledge Network*, 20 April.

Register, R. (1987) *Ecocity Berkeley: Building Cities for a Healthy Future*, Berkeley, CA, North Atlantic Books.

Reichholf, R. J. (2008) *Expert input (Panel 1) to the Conference of Parties to the UN Conference on Biodiversity*, Bonn, Germany May 2008, http://www.iclei.org/index.php?id=6834 (Accessed 15 October 2009).

Scheer, R. (2001) 'Parks as lungs – urban forests and pollution control', *The Environmental Magazine*, November–December.

Taylor, I. (2008) 'Welcome to Eco-city', *BBC Focus*, issue 197, December.

Thames Estuary Partnership (1999) *Management Guidance for the Thames Estuary: Today's Estuary for Tomorrow: Strategy*, http://www.thamesweb.com/tep.php (Accessed 6 October 2009).

TransitionNetwork (n.d.) http://transitiontowns.org (Accessed 20 Nov 2009).

UK Climate Projections (2009) Pre-prepared maps & graphs: UK-wide maps, http://ukclimateprojections.defra.gov.uk/content/view/912/545/ (Accessed 1 December 2009).

Vauban (n.d.) 'Vauban district, Freiburg, Germany', http://www.vauban.de/info/abstract.html (Accessed 16 October 2009).

Vogel, G. (2008) 'Upending the traditional farm', *Science*, vol. 319, 8 February, p. 752.

Warren, J. (2009) 'Corporate responsibility in practice: building an eco-city from scratch', in *Environment, Development and Sustainability: perspectives and cases from around the world*, Oxford University Press and the Open University.

Worldwatch Institute (2007) Preface to *State of the World 2007: Our Urban Future*, New York, Norton and Co.

Acknowledgements

Grateful acknowledgement is made to the following sources:

Text

Page 109 Box 2.5: © Rocky Mountain Institute; Page 133: Poole, R. (2007) A Tale of two Cities, *Engineering and Technology*, The Institution of Engineering and Technology; Pages 136 to 139: Taylor, I. (2008) Welcome to eco-city, *BBC Focus magazine*, Issue 197, Dec 2008, BBC Magazines Bristol Ltd; Page 137: Image © ARUP; Page 143 Box 3.1: From www.livingroofs.org; Page 149: Moore, R. (2009) Vertical Gardens: the Height of Fashion, *London Evening Standard*, 18th May 2009, Solo Syndication Ltd; Page 128: Taken from www.globalpublicmedia.com; Page 173: McCarthy, M. (2008) Mystery of the vanishing sparrow, *The Independent*, 20 Nov 2008. Photo by David Sannison; Page 182: © Crown Copyright 2009, the Meteorological Office; Page 185: Frost, R. The Road not Taken, Henry Holt and Company.

Figures

Figure 1.1a: © iStockphoto; Figure 1.1b: © PhotoDisc; Figure 1.1c: © Getty Images; Figure 1.1d: © picturesbyrob/Alamy; Figures 1.2a, b and 1.3b: From Batty, M. et al. (2008) The Size, Scale and Shape of Cities, *Science*, © AAAS; Figure 1.2c: Image courtesy of Earth Sciences and Image Analysis Laboratory, NASA Johnson Space Center at http://eol.jsc.nasa.gov; Figure 1.6: Adapted from White, H.P. (1963) *A Regional History of Railways* Vol III Greater London, Orion Publishing Group Ltd; Figures 1.7, 1.9, 1.16, 1.18c, 1.20, 1.24, 1.25, 1.31a, 1.31b: Courtesy of Dr Bob Everett; Figure 1.8: Over London - By Rail, from 'London, a Pilgrimage', written by William Blanchard Jerrold (1826-94), engraved by Stephane Pannemaker (1847-1930), pub. 1872 (engraving), Dore, Gustave (1832-83) © Central Saint Martins College of Art and Design, London/The Bridgeman Art Library; Figure 1.12: © Mary Evans Picture Library; Figure 1.13: © Science Photo Library; Figure 1.14a: Reproduced with permission of Punch Ltd., www.punch.co.uk; Figure 1.14b: © Mary Evans Picture Library; Figure 1.17: Mary Evans Picture Library/Mary Evans ILN Pictures; Figure 1.18a: Mary Evans Picture Library/Grosvenor Prints; Figure 1.18b: © Mary Evans Picture Library; Figure 1.19: Courtesy of Thames Water; Figures 1.21 and 1.22: © Mary Evans Picture Library; Figure 1.23: Taken from www.flickr.com. Photo by www.photos8.com and used under http://creativecommons.org/licenses/by/2.0/deed.en_GB; Figure 1.25: Courtesy of Chartered Institution of Building Services Engineers Heritage Group; Figure 1.26: © National Gallery Picture Library; Figures 1.27 and 1.30: Brimblecombe, P. (1986) *The Big Smoke: A History of Air Pollution in London Since Medieval Times*, Routledge; Figure 1.28: © Mary Evans Picture Library; Figures 1.29 and 1.32: © Getty Images; Figure 1.33a: © Mary Evans Picture Library / Chris Coupland; Figure 1.33b: © Mary Evans Picture Library / Illustrated London News; Figures 1.34 and 1.35: Adapted from: *50 years on: The Struggle for Air Quality in London Since the Great Smog of December 1952* (2002), Greater London Authority.